Dark

Psychology

The Final Collection to Learn Dark Psychology

(The Dark Manual to Decipher and Manipulate the Threads of Body Language)

Jude Crowe

Published By **John Kembery**

Jude Crowe

*Dark Psychology: The Final Collection to Learn
Dark Psychology (The Dark Manual to Decipher
and Manipulate the Threads of Body Language)*

ISBN   978-1-9992826-8-4

Legal & Disclaimer

The information contained in this book is not designed to replace or take the place of any form of medicine or professional medical advice. The information in this book has been provided for educational & entertainment purposes only.

The information contained in this book has been compiled from sources deemed reliable, and it is accurate to the best of the Author's knowledge; however, the Author cannot guarantee its accuracy and validity and cannot be held liable for any errors or omissions. Changes are periodically made to this book. You must consult your doctor or get professional medical advice before using any of the suggested remedies, techniques, or information in this book.

Table Of Contents

Chapter 1: The Many Faces Of Manipulation

2.1 Emotional Manipulation: The Puppet Master's Strings

At its center, emotional manipulation is prepared controlling someone emotionally thru persuasion or coercion. Imagine yourself because the fortress; emotional manipulators are like sneaky invaders who use worry-mongering procedures and emotional blackmail to drawbridge down yourself voluntarily - exploiting fears, objectives and smooth spots to transport you into positions that benefit them and in no way reason you any real misery - from time to time without you even identifying it happening on the begin; often taking on roles of worrying friend or lover at the identical time as manipulating feelings to govern you need a human joystick!

Let's find out some real-existence examples. Have you ever skilled roommates who leave dishes piling up, only with a purpose to lose your temper and ask why, they would flip the tables and accuse you of overreacting and being overly emotional while confronted? That is an effective tactic known as emotional manipulation! Or how about romantic partners who display awesome care at some degree in the 'honeymoon section,' excellent frequently fade out as time is going on - fundamental you to question yourself as someone needy or paranoid at the same time as confronted - certain - that too counts!

Such procedures can cause giant damage over the long term. They're like an unseen however gradual leak eroding the integrity of a stone sink; their cumulative consequences may be disastrous. A manipulator might not absolutely drain your emotional reserves - they could slowly put on away at your enjoy of self really absolutely well worth as well, predominant to debilitating conditions like anxiety and depression, which in turn impact exquisite relationships and careers negatively as well.

But why does emotional manipulation strike this shape of chord of stealthiness? Two reasons. First, these manipulators have a propensity to be charismatic and reputedly sympathetic people, drawing you in without understanding what is happening. Second, emotional manipulation does now not discriminate; it can seem everywhere at on every occasion and with honestly everybody-- your mother may be guilty of coercing you into attending own family events that you may rather pass; your terrific friend can also want to usually make plans round their time table making you experience guilty if some thing differs; even your boss may also need to strain extra art work by complimenting for your 'self-discipline' in advance than giving more art work responsibilities!

No want to panic! Don't despair: in later chapters we're capable of offer an arsenal of intellectual self-protection strategies, actionable strategies and boundary putting strategies that allows you to use in opposition to all and sundry who attempts to control or abuse you. We will train you a way to recognize red flags, decode manipulation strategies and grasp the paintings of announcing no without turning into someone's unwitting marionette puppet!

And accept as true with me once I say this: Emotional manipulation is first-class Act One in an complex multi-act play of severa manipulative tactics. Keep a watch constant constant out due to the fact we are about to delve into greater brand new highbrow guidelines, mind video video games and gaslighting processes - accept as true with me; be prepared - this ebook can function your education floor!

2.2 Psychological Tricks and Mind Games

Are you familiar with the phrase, "divide and conquer?" Well, some manipulators use this as their motto - they sow seeds of discord interior businesses so it becomes less complicated for them to manipulate humans. Imagine being aggravated with control at your administrative center; truly certainly one of your colleagues begins offevolved gossiping that people may moreover have already got mystery pay will increase, growing divisions amongst you that allow the manipulator to advantage power via chaos.

Consider projection, an clever mental tactic just like the magic hints completed with the useful resource of David Copperfield. Projection involves manipulators accusing you of doing what they themselves have devoted - as an instance an unfaithful companion accusing you of cheating on the way to divert hobby far from themselves and get you protective over an hassle which must have in no way arisen within the first place! When this tactic works it keeps us focused on our innocence at the same time as in reality forgetting to impeach theirs... Clever!

False quandary is one of the more modern intellectual strategies, designed to strain you into making an adverse desire that advantages them at once. They might also additionally make it appear as even though your rate or commitment are at stake, swaying you toward making their choice instead.

Can we strive 'crazy-making' now? This shape of mind video video games includes changing small elements of fact to make you doubt your self, like when a person denies announcing what became in reality stated or claims they have got achieved some factor they recognize is untrue; you start to doubt yourself and query if fact has end up distorted - creating an emotional vacuum which the manipulator quite really fills by manner of growing their manipulation efforts similarly.

Sometimes human beings have interaction in deceptively diffused passive-aggressive conduct - collectively with at the same time as someone gives assist on a challenge and then drags their ft, causing you to miss remaining dates; or at the same time as their accomplice consents to carry out chores however completes them so poorly you need to redo them your self. When challenged approximately it, their response often leaves you bewildered as they act damage and declare their superb simply isn't always suitable sufficient; you end up accepting blame for their shortcomings alternatively.

Okay, that changed into quite the excursion of a number of the intellectual hints and thoughts video games you can come upon in life - frightening stuff! Don't surrender just however no matter the reality that; we've were given your back right here too. Stay tuned - as in destiny chapters we're capable of unpack more manipulation strategies similarly to provide you with system to fight their strength. So stay with us!

2.Three Gaslighting: Twisting Reality

Imagine being in a dating wherein your companion constantly claims you are forgetful, beginning from small things collectively with "You generally neglect approximately approximately to show off the lighting." Eventually, their claims enhance till they propose you forgot an entire communique that without a doubt befell - leaving you compelled and questioning whether or not or now not memories exist in any respect - leading them to come to be your bypass-to supply for what's "actual" and what isn't "actual." That is gaslighting at play!

Imagine this--you have a friend who's constantly overdue for meetings, regularly arriving 30-forty minutes overdue whenever you join up. However, whilst you supply this hassle up with them they emerge as disillusioned and accuse you of now not appreciating their friendship over some issue so trivial as punctuality. Now you find out yourself questioning whether or not or now not or now not punctuality genuinely is that important--are you being gaslit right proper here? What has really befell proper right here is being gaslighted.

Push it similarly. Now allow's don't forget gaslighting at paintings? That too occurs; accept as true with being given a undertaking with a very quick reduce-off date, strolling throughout the clock to finish it earlier than the lessen-off date arrives first-class to have your boss claim they in no way set it and blame you for dashing and making errors in its completion - suddenly your artwork ethic, memory or even sanity come into query.

Imagine being in an limitless maze wherein every flip leads further from the go out and in the direction of confusion. Gaslighters thrive on preserving you at an uncomfortable equilibrium; in no manner facts whether a few factor actual, imagined, or honest exists - in immoderate cases you could even begin distrusting your self - that is how damaging gaslighting is: it erodes self-remember so successfully that similarly manipulation will become possible.

How are you able to arm your self in competition to gaslighting? I understand this could appear intimidating at the begin, but do not be concerned: as we improvement via this e-book we can talk techniques for recognizing and counteracting gaslighting; find out its highbrow roots; similarly to find out why gaslighters act this manner; I may additionally provide you with highbrow armor so you now not only live on, however thrive!

2.Four Love Bombing: A Dangerous Embrace

Love bombing's seductive attraction has extended been identified. Like an captivating siren's track, love bombing lures humans in with sweet melodies best to leave them heartbroken on emotional turmoil's seashores. If this seems dramatic, it's far due to the fact love bombing itself may be quite dramatic! Let's delve deeper into this manipulative intellectual technique and have a observe its numerous layers as we untangle its many complexities as a manipulative method.

Imagine this: you meet a person who looks as if the whole lot you can ever choice for and additional. They hold close onto every word you say, ship gives that seem drawn straight away out of your dreams, and gush over you need you're the middle of their romantic comedy. Texts come pouring in throughout the clock even as late night time cellular cellphone calls maintain until dawn...And there are candy nothings exchanged throughout those late-night time time mobile phone calls as well! It can experience dizzying however high-quality all on the identical time - like dwelling a fantasy truth in which all is placed and all opportunities. You take within the entire aspect on this fable land wherein simplest divinities exist!

But keep on - why the frenzy? That need to be your first purple flag; love bombing often starts offevolved offevolved speedy and enormously, like an emotional entice being set for you only to be pulled over again out later. This pace of manipulation makes it now not viable if you need to expect or see in truth sufficient for precise judgment to rise up.

What happens psychologically, even though? Love bombing works with the aid of manner of the usage of attractive your mind's reward device - an historical trouble that gives with pleasure and addiction - maximum critical to a rise in dopamine degrees, just like gambling or drug dependancy, making you counting on them in order that after they switch strategies afterward you're more susceptible and open up more successfully to their lows - something they ensure takes vicinity ultimately! This makes love bombers adept at controlling conditions through exploiting our vulnerability while confronted with lows that they understand will come in the end.

And permit's speak that unsightly switcheroo. Once emotionally involved with someone, then their proper sun shades begin to emerge - compliments grow to be passive-aggressive feedback or worse, direct insults; excellent time turns into nonexistent, leaving you disoriented, wondering your self and wondering whether you deserve more--an impact called gaslighting that often accompany love bombing relationships.

Chapter 2: Recognizing The Manipulators In Your Life

three.1 Types of Manipulators: Wolves in Sheep's Clothing

Start off with the useful resource of considering Narcissists: they love themselves, positive; but what they love even greater is control. Their ego thrives off of getting power over others; their desire is to keep dominance. Their international is their universe, and they want you to recognize it using flattery, enchantment or grand gestures--something necessary to maintain their magnetic preserve close over you.

Machiavellians are some other beauty of people. These strategists take into account each interplay a chess exercise; manipulation a pleasant artwork. Friendships turn out to be transactions; love? Dependent upon what may be supplied to them. Machiavellians take into account in justifying method; so if bending or breaking policies becomes essential for their goals, they do no longer hesitate to do it without hesitation.

Don't forget the "Victim." This character makes use of your empathy in opposition to you through using painting themselves because the innocent sufferer in lifestyles's unfairness. Helping them looks as if the right factor to do inside the starting; but fast sufficient you are drawn into an endless cycle of saving them; exploiting your appropriate nature on the same time as making you experience accountable on every occasion trying to set limits or set clean expectancies.

The seducer is some different conventional manipulator. They do not simply romance you; they seduce with terms, movements and bodily attributes to lure you of their internet and make you enjoy precise and understood; all while manipulating you into giving them what they want in go back.

Gaslighters need to in no way be ignored, each. These human beings are grasp manipulators thru sowing seeds of doubt approximately your notion and sanity - for example arguing that the sky is surely green until you start questioning its existence in truth - using deception to gain electricity over you and keep them beneath their thumb.

Just wow - that modified into pretty an remarkable lineup! Of direction, not each character who exhibits the ones trends intends to manipulate your life; humans can act differently due to past opinions, emotional triggers or pressure of the moment - the secret's recognizing the ones styles and protective your self because it should be.

3.2 Tactics They Use: The Methods to the Madness

Now which you are familiar with the manipulators rogue's gallery, permit's delve deeper into their toolbox of strategies they employ in their manipulation efforts. Recognizing their identity is simplest half of of the battle; to correctly combat their actions you want an expertise of their strategies; so permit's smash down their techniques; some can be honestly as cunning as foxes among henhouses!

Let's begin our exploration with "Love Bombing." At first, this will sound appealing; until you understand it's miles sincerely an complicated entice set by using using manipulators. They shower you with affection, objects and too much interest until they hook you; as soon as this has happened even though, their plan becomes obvious; their purpose? To make you so based upon their affection that you have a study their goals with the intention to hold feeling cherished.

"Triangulation," some other common manipulation tactic, involves inclusive of some different individual into the combination in an effort to energy you in the direction of them and push away your partner - growing jealousy or lack of self guarantee among you , essential you to vie with every specific for his or her affection no matter now not agreeing on such phrases earlier than.

"Negging" may be an insidious exercise. This shape of manipulation utilizes backhanded compliments or subtle criticisms designed to undermine your experience of self, so as for the manipulator to gain authority through manipulating you into seeking out validation from them - in conjunction with comments together with, "You are so smart for now not attending college" or "You appearance stunning at the identical time as absolutely attempting."

Have you heard of "Bait and Switch"? People will make ensures but then make genuine on handiest half of of. This takes place in jobs even as promised promotions don't materialize and relationships at the same time as emotional manual disappears as soon as a person secures your dedication.

Ouch! Don't overlook the traditional exercising of gaslighting. These human beings will project your memory of sports activities, make untrue claims approximately you saying assets you did not, and normally purpose doubt as to whether or not or not or not or no longer you're crazy - all with one purpose in thoughts: undermining self warranty in your very personal judgment to stress you into deferring to theirs as an alternative.

Are You Spotting the Pattern Here? Manipulators purpose your emotional and intellectual nicely-being to their benefit, know-how that once they get you doubting your self they are able to step in as a savior you rely on for resource - almost like hacking into your mental mainframe itself! Once conscious, however, you may located up strong defenses towards those intellectual invaders.

three.Three Red Flags: The Tell-tales Signs

If someone changes their behavior like a chameleon on a rainbow, that could be a trademark that they will be trying to manipulate you or hold you guessing as to their intentions. By retaining you guessing and disorienting you so rapid, manipulators are retaining their mark off balance so it may be difficult for others to look at what their proper motives can be.

Next is "Too Much, Too Soon". Everyone enjoys a brief-paced romance story, however if someone is pushing too difficult for emotional or financial commitments too soon then take be conscious - they'll be seeking to rush you into making choices you have not without a doubt considered however.

Keep a be careful for "Isolation Tactics." If they start guidance you faraway from pals and family, warning bells ought to sound immediately. Their intention? To become your primary supply of records, advice, or social interaction; with a lot a great deal much less enter from others comes lots less manage over your worldview.

Don't forget about "Passive-Aggressive Behavior." Whether it is diffused backhanded compliments, sarcasm, or guarantees made then damaged, passive aggressiveness is a covert shape of manipulate used to exert authority without direct war of phrases - almost like intellectual conflict!

How often have you ever ever witnessed a person gambling "The Victim" in each state of affairs? If someone continues portraying themselves as sufferers notwithstanding evidence to the other, it can be used as a manipulation tactic through making you revel in responsible and forcing you to make amends despite the fact that there was no wrongdoing in your element!

Here's a tough one: "Lying thru Omission." Not telling you the complete tale may be in reality as deceitful, with those keep close manipulators being adept at the use of partial truths to craft narratives tailor-made specially to their desires.

Be wary inside the event that they appear cause on "Shifting the Blame." Did they lessen to rubble? Still your fault. These Teflon masters make sure now not a few thing sticks to them, leaving you to wallow in guilt or confusion on the identical time as their hands remain easy.

Chapter 3: The Inner Workings Of Nlp

4.1 What is NLP and Why It Matters

So allow's dispose of some of this jargon. "Neuro" refers to your mind and the way it translates sensory enter, inclusive of what your five senses stumble upon and the way they understand some factor new. Next comes "Linguistics," now not restricted to words coming out of your mouth but consisting of gestures, posture and eye actions in addition to silence among phrases. Finally "Programming" does no longer speak over with coding in step with se but greater like how those studies and selections get hardwired into behavior styles through hardwiring them for your brain, almost like writing intellectual software program!

Assuming you apprehend, but thinking "So, why all the fuss?" You might be right; allow us to complicated further. NLP is extra than an educational idea: it is able to decode how we technique reviews, effect selections, and modify emotional responses - which makes it awesome in its very own right - however like every tool it is able to moreover be misused for each suitable and unwell purposes.

NLP can be a quite useful remedy tool. Imagine being capable of rewrite your inner "code" to alleviate phobias or boom conceitedness settings so you can with a chunk of achievement walk into any room such as you very own it! NLP moreover performs an crucial problem in organization worldwide environments - ever been surprised at salespeople that appear capable of have a look at your thoughts? They can be the use of NLP strategies if you want to better realise your goals and communicate more efficiently.

At its coronary coronary heart, NLP additionally can be a grasp manipulator's dream toolkit. A skilled practitioner of its techniques can surely harm into your idea techniques to strain out hidden secrets and techniques or convince you to make picks you will no longer typically make - making NLP each effective and threatening all on the identical time! Therefore, being aware of NLP is fundamental; know-how gives the system important for preventing misuse at the same time as imparting you with strength in competition to mental trickeries in modern-day day society.

"But wait! There's greater!" because the infomercials proclaim. NLP has seamlessly transitioned into the digital sphere. You are in all likelihood encountering NLP techniques not sincerely throughout conversations or remedy commands however additionally whilst browsing social media posts, advertisements, or clicking clickbait headlines like the ones boasting "Ten Things Only Smart People Understand." That clickbait headline wasn't magically written - possibilities are, NLP techniques had been hired to engineer it that permits you to attract you in.

My pals, as we discover this rabbit hollow over the subsequent numerous segments, you may benefit a keener eye for identifying NLP in its herbal putting. Imagine carrying magical glasses to look hidden messages and invisible strings; through the surrender of this bankruptcy NLP won't appear so mysterious or daunting a subject; rather you may begin viewing human interplay from precise perspectives; from casual communique to heated debate, recognizing each benign and manipulative practices inside the again of terms is some component you may quickly do instinctively.

Are You Intrigued Yet? Well, You Should Be! Get ready to get to the lowest of this wonderful feat of highbrow perception as your adventure through the thoughts's maze starts to come to be even more fascinating!

4.2 The Pillars of NLP: Representational Systems

Neuro-Linguistic Programming (NLP) takes us deep into its center additives - its Pillars or

"Representational Systems." These foundational systems shape the idea of the manner we recognize, manner, and react to our environment - like operating software program application that keeps your thoughts strolling smoothly. When you recognize the ones pillars you unfastened up an entire international of self-popularity further to possibilities for changing now not certainly behaviors however reviews as nicely.

NLP Representational Systems embody Visual (V), Auditory (A), Kinesthetic (K), Olfactory (O), and Gustatory (G), usually noted thru their acronym VAKOG. Each tool represents one sensory channel via which we revel in lifestyles. Let's damage the ones down step-via-step?

Visual (V) -- Ever heard the adage, "A picture is virtually certainly worth a thousand terms"? Well there may be an tremendous purpose inside the decrease back of it: folks that depend carefully on photos, solar sunglasses and spatial orientation have a tendency to apply images as part of their verbal exchange strategies and thrive when dealing with visual ideas and situations - frequently having robust imaginations themselves!

These human beings would possibly probable say topics inclusive of, "I see what you advise" or "Imagine this", at the same time as the usage of this system effectively should allow them to emerge as masters of persuasion and communique - creating high-quality intellectual snap shots which help have interaction your motive audiences and preserve them entertained and engaged!

Auditory (A) -- Auditory machine human beings are the listeners, folks who discover consolation in song or voices and like receiving records through spoken phrases in preference to published ones. You might probably listen them the use of terms like, "That sounds appropriate" or "Listen to this." Understanding NLP let you master intonation and timing even as speaking - whether or not or no longer to influence, comfort or command your conversational opposite numbers.

Kinesthetic (K) -- Kinesthetic communique includes sensory opinions like touch, emotion and temperature. If you regularly discover yourself announcing things like "That feels right" or "I cannot recognize this concept", then your statistics may additionally lie with K. This information may be vital for bodily obligations in addition to emotional connections - ever observe how a warmth hug or enterprise handshake can right now modify assembly dynamics? That is K communication at its finest!

Olfactory (O) and Gustatory (G) systems - These tons less often cited however however crucial structures talk over with our senses of scent and flavor respectively, each powerful structures related right away to reminiscence and emotion - remembering a heady scent from your teenagers can deliver again amazing reminiscences, on the equal time as precise flavors can cause sturdy emotional responses in our our our bodies. Together those senses can create an unforgettable experience. These senses also can be blended with distinct representational structures for an stepped forward revel in.

Representational Systems are crucial. Think of them like man or woman languages that your thoughts speaks; when you observe which one dominates, you gain the capability to translate reports and information more with out problem and recall it higher. Furthermore, expertise other human beings's primary structures allows you to tailor communication efficaciously so it's going to have maximum effect and persuasive strength.

But wait, there's more! These structures do not represent rigid instructions; as an alternative they represent fluid inclinations that you may teach your mind to replace between as preferred - think about this like becoming multilingual! Imagine all the opportunities this opens up: superior relationships, sharper desire making abilties or even more potent self-focus!

And herein lies the rub: through facts NLP's Pillars of NLP, no longer simplest will you be arming your self in competition to manipulation but you can additionally free up gear to supplement your life in multiple methods. So whether or not it's far blockading easy talkers or impressing all through hobby interviews, understanding Representational Systems can be your thriller weapon for achievement.

four.Three Calibration and Anchoring: Tools or Weapons?

Calibration and Anchoring are just like the Swiss Army knives of NLP: they will be effective device used for every powerful or harmful manipulation of human behavior. Once you observe their secrets, those men emerge as ubiquitous anywhere from marketing campaigns to political speeches - prepared? Let's get going!

"Calibration." Think of calibration because the art of studying human beings like an open ebook--or, higher despite the fact that, like an complex novel. To calibrate, carefully take a look at every verbal and nonverbal cues given off via human beings to benefit insight into their mental or emotional states. Not truely what human beings are saying - alternatively it is how they may be announcing it along any subtle body language indicators collectively with blinks in their eyelids or modifications in posture that provide an correct reading.

Chapter 4: Building A Defensive Fortress

5.1 Setting Emotional Boundaries

Let's be clean about some thing: Boundaries don't advise being remote and advanced; as an alternative, don't forget them more as non-public guidelines for a way your dating capabilities. Just as you will not allow a stranger into your own home and start analyzing your image albums without your permission (if that had been ever to reveal up, we want to talk!) so too want to there be guidelines defining who gets to enter into your emotional vicinity and the way they want to act there.

Still harassed? Allow me to help. Consider your lifestyles like a lovely fortress with stunning gardens, a moat, and excessive walls - this represents every your emotional and intellectual states. Now take into account who want to go into: family? Friends? Your puppy goldfish Gilbert? As gatekeeper of your fort, YOU determine who receives get entry to. Clearly lowering the drawbridge can also entice many but doing so may need to permit in oldsters that might purpose havoc or maybe start fires in your pantry; at the identical time as being too selective ought to depart you searching like an antique hermit with out lots records or cool wizard hats! The key lies in placing a balance: statistics whilst to decrease or maintain up that drawbridge!

Let's remember an instance from practicality: Say you are at a own family dinner at the equal time as Uncle Joe starts offevolved wondering why you are single, childless or do no longer however make million. In the vintage you may have answered in pain through the usage of way of imparting indistinct motives or converting the situation; not so with you presently which have emotional armor to set limitations with out issues - alternatively telling him in a polite manner however firmly that his inquiry into your private affairs are personal topics and you do not want to speak approximately them publicly right now; now with you know-how this skillful you location barriers like an expert! Congratulations; putting limitations like an professional!

Imagine this: you have a chum who likes to apply late-night time conversations as an outlet for their ongoing drama, so while matters end up hard for you they appear overextended. Unfortunately even as you need someone, whilst their problems become your troubles they become busy as hell - once they be conscious an imbalance it is able to be time to set obstacles; permit them to recognize you want to live supportive but have positive expectations of them themselves.

And do no longer get me began on art work - in case you discover yourself burning the midnight oil, answering emails during own family food, or lowering excursion quick for conferences scheduled very last minute then Houston, we've were given a boundary trouble! Remember you're an employee with existence outdoor the administrative center; therefore it could be useful to meet along with your boss or HR to set up boundaries for your availability and set limits on at the identical time as you need to be to be had for paintings.

5.2 Mental Self-Defense Techniques

Once we've got set up the emotional obstacles, permit's discuss highbrow self-protection techniques to guard ourselves in opposition to highbrow assaults from others. Let's face it; existence can now and again be tough and those who are seeking for to undermine your intellectual properly being might also try their good fortune at entering into.

Grab your pocket ebook or truely pay near attention, due to the truth we are going to delve into an arsenal of intellectual self-safety strategies to get us going! Let's dive in!

Technique #1: The Power of No"

A unmarried phrase? Absolutely actual. Saying no can be like having a further safety defend to your arsenal. Think returned on all the ones instances you stated "yes" while surely you preferred to scream "NO!," like while your neighbor asked you for doggy sitting yet again or your boss wanted you to art work over the weekend--pronouncing no is more than genuinely verbal; it's far putting forward your private limits via setting an important boundary between what's ideal and unacceptable, as a end result saying to human beings, basically announcing, 'this is my line, don't move it."

But I apprehend: announcing no can be hard, specially when you have a bent to be human beings-pleaser. You could probably feel as even though you're letting someone down or coming across as unkind; in reality despite the fact that, it is probably more unkind within the course of your self to maintain saying superb whilst your real purpose is not any. A no might now not commonly mean "I hate you", it without a doubt method: I value my time, strength and resources and pick out out how quality to spend them.

Technique #2: The Gray Rock Method

Imagine yourself as an unassuming gray rock rather than being the type that draws hobby and grabs human beings's hobby, like sparkling stones do. Why may sincerely all and sundry do this type of detail, you ask? Well, this strategy may be very beneficial while managing manipulative or overly aggressive humans, who thrive off your reactions -- like emotional vampires who feed off of anger, frustration and unhappiness to thrive themselves!

To combat them correctly you switch out to be as silly and inactive as a grey stone would possibly.

Sounds loopy, I understand; but it works! Just permit them to speak, rant or strive to pull you into their emotional hurricane; stay detached by using way of imparting monosyllabic responses or just nodding your head occasionally. Soon sufficient they'll tire of talking or begin looking someplace else for sparkling meat to eat; remember it as turning into in brief emotionally invisible!

Technique #three: Creating a Mental Buffer Zone

Imagine this: you are engaged in an emotionally charged discussion or dispute and a person begins offevolved throwing emotional jabs your way. Instead of taking every blow head-on, create a highbrow buffer sector as an imaginary stress field that filters out negativity. How? Simply: Before responding to what they may be announcing, take a deep breath in advance than responding and see if their feedback reflect extra on them and no longer you in my view.

By giving yourself time and place for idea, you're growing a highbrow barrier that offers you a chance to answer in preference to react. Reacting is emotional whilst responding is rational. Your buffer sector enables make sure you remain interior this latter realm wherein manipulate over consequences exists.

Technique #four: Reality Testing

Have you been experiencing a person seeking out to gaslight you or make you doubt your non-public research? Reality Testing can help. Whenever some component seems off, take a minute or so to evaluate whether or not or no longer what has been told is accurate; or is some element being left unsaid that contradicts with what become being recommended to you? Depending on how unsure you revel in, ask a relied on friend their opinion as nicely if need be.

Chapter 5: The Unspoken Dialogue

6.1 The Basics: What Your Body is saying?

Let's pass deeper into body language, an unstated form of discussion that regularly says more than any terms ever ought to. Why does this depend? Simply because of the truth body language no longer regularly lies; agree with this nonverbal soundtrack accompanying each social come upon and choosing up on subtleties you'll no longer normally be conscious.

Have you ever walked right into a room and right now felt tension rise up round you, like it may reduce via with a knife? No magic right here; it actually is frame language at play. Clenched fists, pursed lips, prevented eyes-- these diffused cues ship clear messages about ache, anxiety or hostility in an surroundings. Understanding body language not quality permits you to interpret the vibe of any given environment but moreover offers a useful degree for gauging human beings sincerity; understanding it gives you with a further revel in that lets in detecting indicators that in any other case would possibly bypass neglected.

Now, I apprehend what you're thinking: "Cool idea, but how do I in truth get top at this?" Here's wherein it receives thrilling: tap into your internal Sherlock Holmes and start looking. Pay near hobby to the whole thing from small twitches and microexpressions to even the pace of someone's breathing as those can all provide clues. Don't pass whole-on detective mode really but - instead turn out to be privy to those small actions human beings perform subconsciously.

Make no mistake--your frame speaks volumes too! As you navigate the arena round you, take heed to any signals being transmitted with the aid of yourself: crossed palms have to come off as defensive or closed off; gambling with hair may also need to signal tension or flirtation. Everything from the way you occupy area, the expansiveness of posture or tilt of head are quantities that others can also be seeking out to recognize.

Why is frame language studying specially essential whilst carried out to manipulation and darkish psychology? Let me ruin it down for you: manipulators are masters at analyzing frame language. They pick out up on cues you unknowingly deliver and use them toward you for their private benefit. Imagine entering into a immoderate-stakes negotiation: having knowledge of a few different birthday celebration's body language must offer you with the threshold; as an example recognizing signs of anxiety or insecurity have to supply an pinnacle hand benefit whilst projecting an air of self guarantee might also want to create an unspoken area - they'll deliver an unstated gain without them understanding.

Mastering body language offers you with a effective social X-ray vision, allowing you to peer thru human beings's facades and get to the center of their intentions. But this is simply the cease of the iceberg; our frame language journey continues past this component, from deception cues to electricity dynamics; so keep tight, this need to be an thrilling trip!

6.2 Reading Faces: Windows to the Soul

If you've got completed poker, possibilities are you have got heard of a "poker face." This time period refers to an expression used while no emotion ought to come through; while one desires to appear impartial. Unfortunately in lifestyles maximum humans fail at keeping such expressions; their faces display screen emotions they'll in no way particular verbally.

Have you ever met a person and were given the texture that something wasn't quite proper with them? Maybe their jaw became tightened, their eyebrow subtly raised or lips barely curled were telltale signs and symptoms that some thing wasn't pretty proper? Even at the same time as their phrases said one factor, their faces may additionally have cautioned you some different message--saying both "Hey! This is not okay with me!" or "Yes, you have got got my complete interest!" Facial muscle mass can produce over 7,000 splendid expressions--take into account all of the emotional insights they could offer! If that have become not noted...

Interpreting facial cues may also moreover furthermore seem honest inside the starting, however interpretation can be complex at the same time as taken in context. Squinted eyes ought to imply suspicion in a unmarried scenario whilst signaling a person left their reading glasses at domestic in every other placing. It's key to cluster observations; touching their face regularly at the same time as talking ought to suggest pain or dishonesty on the same time as coupled with particular incongruent behaviors like moving gaze and worried fidgeting.

Now, I wager you're thinking how this all ties again into manipulators and dark psychology. Get prepared for a shock: manipulators frequently own an super potential to keep an now not effects seen facade; those human beings have perfected the art work of preserving quiet but commonly have one or greater tells which exposes their genuine identities - often via diffused facial cues that require keen observation from an eagle eye for facial cues; finding those flaws might not come effortlessly - masters of disguise have one or extra flaws which display their identities - you virtually want to find out in which this one lies!

At the same time as analyzing others, preserve in thoughts that your face is your billboard too. Being greater aware about how your expressions form the affect that others get of you is essential to controlling how others see you. Ever study charismatic human beings often have lively, expressive faces? They leverage facial cues to connect, interact and effect - the usage of facial expressions for connection, engagement and have an impact on; you may do the same through powerful, sincere communication - the use of facial capabilities to intensify phrases, display empathy or engage is an awesome social toolkit device!

Faces are the Grand Central Station of emotional transit, so studying to examine them nicely is essential in relationships, commercial enterprise or even shielding oneself from manipulation. You are not really mastering about faces; as a substitute you're reading intentions, motivations and hidden agendas of people you encounter every day.

6.Three Power Poses Are A Hidden Arsenal

Now that you've grow to be adept at reading faces, allow's shift gears and discover some element absolutely invigorating: electricity poses! How you stand or sit down down isn't always only for consolation or etiquette; it is able to sincerely have a super impact on how others view and understand you. No kidding-this stuff works: studies shows adopting energy poses can truely exchange body chemistry via the use of growing self belief at the equal time as reducing stress--who knew?!?

Imagine this: Imagine you're approximately to walk into an interview, date or any scenario in that you want to offer your fine self. What are you doing earlier than moving into this case? Hunching over your telephone with shoulders slumped down or fame tall with shoulders over again exuding self guarantee? Interestingly enough, recognition up straighter not handiest makes you seem more assured; it simply improves how assured you experience - developing a remarks loop amongst frame and mind as real as any device used for reading this text.

Assume for a 2d that manipulators exude self belief. By adopting an assertive stance and projecting it once more at them, manipulators can also appear confident sufficient to assume manage of any vicinity they occupy; every now and then without a doubt with their posture on my own! Faking it until you are making it is an artwork shape they masterfully observe; you could also leverage this towards them through adopting an authoritative posture of your very very personal to installation dominance over them! But with the resource of adopting such an empowering stance in opposition to those puppeteers you can construct resilience at the equal time as sending signals that show them who's boss - let them attempt their tactics on a person much less informed!

However, frame language recognition is going a long way past honestly puffing your chest and pretending to be a superhero--however the truth that that does sound a laugh! Instead, it calls for being aware about the diffused methods your frame language communicates power dynamics. Leaning in at some stage in conversations signals hobby and engagement even as eye contact establishes receive as actual with; at the same time as taking on vicinity - whether or not or not or now not with the aid of way of using spreading fingers during a conference desk or reputation with ft apart--is used as an assertive presence declaration and might guard from manipulation. These poses turn out to be your thriller guns that assist beautify social interactions whilst defensive you in opposition to manipulation!

Chapter 6: Practical Nlp For Self-Defense

7.1 Mindful Listening: Your First Line of Defense

Have everyone ever discovered ourselves engaged in conversations wherein as an opportunity of really listening, our focus has shifted in the path of formulating our next statement? Perhaps accountable as charged? You're Not by myself - aware listening's strength lies exactly in its functionality to break this cycle.

Mindful listening need to not be understood in its conventional enjoy: as passively taking in words from someone else. Instead, conscious listening includes actively and purposefully listening with an alert but open thoughts to truly draw near now not simply the phrases being spoken but their emotional undertones and any hidden agendas lurking underneath - an hobby humans are adept at doing!

Mindful listening can act like a digital armor: thru using it, you lessen the opportunities of manipulators sneaking their mental tips beyond you. Contrarian be aware: did you understand that professional manipulators often hide their intentions through vague language, double meanings, or emotional tones that struggle? But aware listeners can with out problems hit upon such inconsistencies!

How does conscious listening art work? Imagine talking with someone who is lavishing you with reward approximately your modern day achievements - all sounds exquisite so far, proper? However, if their tone or body language shows disdain in your statements or suggests indifference from their issue, conscious listening lets in you to discover any discrepancies - much like having an in-built lie detector!

Mindful listening can become even extra effective even as mixed with insightful questioning. Asking open-ended questions that force a manipulator to expose greater than predicted. For instance, a person would possibly try to gaslight you via saying things like, "You're overreacting; no person else sees this problem." A conscious listener should respond with the useful resource of the usage of asking "What makes you're saying that? Can you hard?" This forces them out in their scripted narrative and forces them to suppose on their ft - scoring one for the quality men!

Let's delve deeper: aware listening permits you to have a look at most of the strains. This technique being attentive to what's not being stated; together with, for instance, omissions, silences and hesitations. For example, if someone often avoids answering direct questions or skillfully adjustments subjects with out warning your aware listening alarm must sound with urgency.

Practice makes ideal, like wine growing older to perfection. Start small; workout at some stage in much less important conditions like circle of relatives dinners or looking political interviews, noting any inconsistencies amongst terms, tone, and frame language -

while you come to be greater adept, you can surprise how you ever managed without it! As quickly as your know-how will increase you can surprise the way you ever controlled without it!

7.2 Spotting Linguistic Patterns: Words as Clues

Consider conscious listening your first line of protection; then flip spotting linguistic styles into your intel operation, your covert reconnaissance assignment. Here is in which you get to play detective and collect clues and build a mean photo of the situation.

Let's soar proper in through discussing some thing you can have heard of but possibly have now not idea plenty about: presuppositions. Presuppositions are assumptions or ideals hidden within sentences - together with at the same time as someone asks, "Why do you constantly lessen to rubble?" which includes an implicit presupposition about why you do 'usually reduce to rubble,' at the same time as that announcement hardly ever holds up as fact. Crafty manipulators use language patterns like this one to plant disempowering beliefs at the equal time as asking an innocent query! But the ones tuned in sufficient will locate it fast enough.

Now allow's turn our awareness to qualifying terms. Statements consisting of 'without a doubt,' 'most effective," or "really" can serve to restrict or trivialize what a person is claiming; as an example if a person tells you "You're sincerely too sensitive," using qualifying terms together with these is probably supposed to downplay or trivialize their emotions - deciding on up on this may supply a trademark that someone might be in search of to restrict either your experience or their non-public actions.

Let's add every other element of complexity and speak indistinct language. Manipulators use it as a smokescreen; phrases that lack specificity at the side of, "Everyone thinks you're overreacting," or "It's all your fault" are phrases manipulators love to use and may sow self-doubt and motive self-loathing. But at the identical time as skilled in spotting the ones styles, disturbing clarity can strip away this veil of mystery.

Feeling intrigued? Stay with us due to the fact there may be one greater trick up our sleeve: double bind. Here, the manipulator creates an impasse in which every doing or now not doing can result in terrible results - for instance: being knowledgeable "If you sincerely cared about me, you will comprehend what is incorrect." Here the manipulator places you into an apparent lose-lose situation in which asking what is incorrect can look like displaying loss of care, while thru no longer asking, well it appears even a good deal an awful lot much less so! Double binds are like manipulative ninja movements; however, recognizing the ones techniques gives you an opportunity to disarm them swiftly earlier than they spread further!

Are You Feeling the Weight? This facts isn't truly juicy; it is actionable intelligence. Once you song into those patterns, it's miles like having X-Ray imaginative and prescient; you could see via all of the fluff and trickery without delay to its motive inside the back of phrases - now, in preference to really being attentive to; you are understanding on a deeper level!

But I understand this is lots to soak up; take into account this as ongoing training for a marathon in vicinity of dash. While mastery will take time and practice, sincerely information those linguistic strategies exist considerably improves your protection exercise.

Words may be greater than mere method of conversation: inside the fingers of manipulators they end up guns that may be applied in competition to you and you. But thru statistics language evaluation you may turn terms from weapons into gear you could use to guard yourself and note through any facades supplied earlier than you.

7.Three Reframing: Turn the Tables

As you could have guessed by means of now, emotional judo is like emotional judo: the usage of the manipulator's very personal strain in competition to them to take again manage and redefine the game. By changing views or the focus of conversations you now not terrific regain electricity but can prevent manipulative strategies useless in their tracks.

So what precisely is reframing? Imagine yourself as an artist, holding onto an extremely good painting however framing it inappropriately with an ugly body that does not do it justice; its functionality glory stays unrealized. Reframing consists of choosing an opportunity body which complements and showcases your masterpiece's capability glory; on this instance we are speakme about conditions, statements or ideals in region of artwork!

Imagine this: your co-employee regularly makes disparaging feedback approximately your punctuality, such as, "Oh, aren't you on time these days? What's the occasion?" Your preliminary reaction is probably defensiveness or contamination; as an alternative, try transferring their focus via responding, "Being punctual is my norm, not an exception. What made you word these days?" Now they non-public their narrative in region of you!

Reframing is not just about dodging bullets; it may additionally boom your internal panorama. When self-doubt or horrible wondering has you down, reframing may be an invaluable supply of treatment. Instead of questioning "Why does awful stuff normally show as an awful lot as me," ask your self "What can I examine from this situation?" Once finished, the scenario now not has the energy to pull you down; as an alternative it will become an opportunity for increase and facts.

Reframing also can be used to undertaking widely regular however probably damaging ideals, just like the ones associated with the traditional "glass ceiling". Instead of accepting it as an insurmountable barrier, keep in thoughts reframing it as a ladder you could climb to break through that ceiling - turning a defeating story into one full of opportunities and empowerment.

Are You Wondering How to Implement Reframing in Your Life? Just Like Dancing

Reframing might be your ultimate intellectual self-protection tool. Versatile, efficiency, and transformative, it now not best combats manipulation but fundamentally alters the manner you have interaction with it too - such an impactful way to stage up!

As we delve into greater superior strategies and gear in destiny chapters, reframing is greater than a tactic; it is a manner of life choice. Reframing fosters highbrow agility and flexibility to assist people now not really continue to exist however thrive in cutting-edge world of manipulation and thoughts video games.

Chapter 7: The Physiology Of Manipulation

eight.1 How Stress Makes Us Susceptible

Are You Susceptible To Manipulation Perhaps pressure has not whatever to do with manipulation, but permit me assure you it does; those bypass hand-in-hand in a sinister dance that could have disastrous results for every. Stress plays recommendations on our brains at the same time as manipulators use every possibility available to them to perform magic pointers on us all.

As we start this talk on pressure and the manner it influences our brains, allow's first define what takes place underneath pressure: your thoughts turns on its "fight or flight" response: adrenaline surges, heartbeat speeds up and blood rushes to muscle corporations - exquisite for outrunning bears but a good buy an awful lot much less splendid even as looking to rationalize alternatives - but this rapid muzzles your prefrontal cortex (the detail responsible for exact judgment, decision-making and strength of mind); you may as properly transfer over to "Safe Mode".

As you grapple with internal chaos, an surprising houseguest abruptly enters: Mr. Or Ms. Manipulator. Like sharks smelling blood in the water, those manipulators fast choose out your inclined spots in advance than springing their plans; guilt journeys, twisting your terms or outrageous desires come quick as a end result - making their challenge a protracted manner easier! It's like selecting a lock whilst its tumblers have already been misaligned; their manner will become a incredible deal much less complicated while seeking to pressure get right of entry to via misalignments in among lock tumblers at the same time as their process will become lots much less difficult!

Never assume in-the-moment stress on my own locations you at risk - chronic stress, the silent creeper, is further adverse. Over time it wears down your highbrow defenses like water wears away rock. At first you could no longer take a look at its effect; however in the long run a canyon workplace work underneath you and an exploitative individual takes gain of your vulnerabilities and begins controlling you from there on out.

Stress makes us prone to developing horrible conduct and loops. For instance, while careworn out you may flip to toxic relationships for help however best emerge as finding that their manipulation compounds your suffering similarly! It's like looking an overheated canine chase its tail - great this time it's miles you feeling the warm temperature!

Be snug: Being aware of this unholy alliance amongst pressure and susceptibility to manipulation places you beforehand of the sport. Unraveling it, allows us to strengthen defenses and maintain that castle we've got were given been building for the duration of this e-book; like having a burglar alarm that not wonderful signals at the identical time as thieves try to gain get entry to but additionally warns when they may be genuinely casing the joint!

eight.2 Fight, Flight, or Freeze: Your Body's Response

After exploring how stress makes us at risk of manipulation, permit's delve deep into "Fight, Flight or Freeze: Your Body's Response." Let's communicate precisely what takes vicinity in our bodies whilst the stress alarm goes off - beyond easy biology; this guide serves as an in-intensity examination of strategies manipulators use recommendations like this one to take over our responses.

Imagine this: even as strolling alongside an alley and being attentive to footsteps coming close to from at the back of, your instantaneous reaction might be each "Run away!" or to expose spherical and confront any functionality threat; others may in all likelihood turn around and confront stated danger; but others can also need to freeze as deer in headlights. Unfortunately, this combat-flight-or-freeze reaction doesn't in truth observe in life-or-loss of lifestyles situations; your nervous device should not distinguish among an real predator lurking nearby and someone seeking to govern you emotionally or psychologically - for your concerned machine, threats exist irrespective of who the deliver can be; consequently your frame reacts for this reason.

Manipulators can find out those physiological modifications - it's miles as although your frame releases pressure hormones like cortisol and adrenaline which, as soon as launched, flood your system with strain hormones that sign "I'm inclined! Take benefit!" They word your sweaty palms, wavering voice, and darting eyes; correctly giving them get admission to in your emotional u . S . - some thing they use to their advantage to speedy take advantage of.

Assuming you input a "combat" mode, your herbal tendency is probably to say your self assertively and stand your floor - however a professional manipulator may additionally moreover need to show this in competition to you with the resource of the usage of gambling victim, prompting doubt in your self and moving blame onto them in choice to you because the aggressor. Now, you're the villain, and your fight has backfired spectacularly. In "flight" mode, your instinct may be to break out the state of affairs as soon as feasible. But the manipulator, being an emotional hunter, might also furthermore interpret your hesitation as evidence of guilt and enhance their processes to make you even worse. And in case you freeze up altogether, they see it as an invitation to push obstacles and exert control without your being capable of intrude or prevent them.

But how are we able to wreck free of this physiological entice? Firstly, apprehend what is happening: is your coronary heart racing sooner or later of an issue, or your palms sweaty at the same time as an sudden assembly arises from work? These signs and symptoms advocate your body going into defensive mode; as quickly as aware of this reality, use counter strategies as rapid as possible - we are able to explore greater in subsequent sections! Simply positioned: arm your self with popularity and techniques that redecorate you from prey into unstoppable forces: positive- you heard me right- you're the hero of this tale!

8.Three Hormones: The Chemical Messengers

Understandably, they could act as unwitting accomplices to manipulators who understand the way to paintings the system.

Let's begin with cortisol, generally referred to as the "pressure hormone." Your adrenal glands launch this chemical at the same time as you experience improved pressure or hazard, but its manufacturing is predicated upon on many particular variables. Herein lies its complexity. Cortisol isn't definitely associated with pressure; it plays an essential characteristic in lots of capabilities consisting of metabolism law and immune response. Cortisol modified into designed as an resource throughout "fight or flight" situations that prepare us for quick motion. Cortisol performs an important characteristic in our physical properly-being; at the identical time as persistent pressure enters, but, cortisol tiers exchange extensively and start to intrude with cognitive skills like reminiscence and interest.

Constant pressure makes people forgetful and masses a good deal much less attentive - some thing manipulators recognize all too properly about.

Dopamine, the critical element player in your mind's praise circuit, has arrived! Remember how superb it feels at the same time as you chunk into an irresistibly scrumptious piece of chocolate or acquire an consist of from someone pricey? That is dopamine at paintings! Released throughout pleasing conditions, dopamine releases emotions of enjoyment and reinforcement, however what takes region at the same time as a person manipulates this system? Aha! Now all of it makes experience!

When manipulators use love-bombing techniques like love bombing to prompt your dopamine circuitry - making you crave their presence and approval at the same time as growing dependency traps with one man or woman being the deliver. Just like getting hooked on capsules - except right here the person does no longer always have your quality interests at coronary coronary heart!

Oxytocin, normally known as the "cuddle hormone", plays an crucial position in social bonding, maternal behaviors and pair bonding - it creates that heat fuzzy feeling even as snuggling near with cherished ones. Trust and empathy ranges increase at the same time as this hormone is launched thru manipulators who capitalize on it via hugging, compliments and gestures timed flawlessly to trick your thoughts into generating extra oxytocin - like puppeteers who apprehend which strings to drag that allows you to instill feelings of consolation and protection of their aim topics.

"Great, so how do I fight biochemical puppetry?" Here's the plan. Awareness need to be your first line of protection in phrases of stopping biochemical puppetry; with the resource of being privy to how those hormones effect your judgment, corrective steps can begin being taken proper away. When feeling too emotionally invested or overstressed, mindfulness techniques can be deployed to distance oneself and compare conditions objectively - or specialists can also offer coping strategies as more guide.

Therefore, what we've got visible up to now is an extraordinary feat: you're not genuinely taking a peek backstage however certainly dismantling it. By turning into adept at recognising and records biochemical responses on your frame, in addition to manipulators's capability abuse of them thru manipulators; subsequent on our journey may be exploring hard thoughts techniques which manipulators are not in all likelihood to need us to understand.

Chapter 8: Navigating The Virtual Minefield

nine.1 Social Media: A Playground for Manipulators

Social media may be likened to an complicated maze with trapdoors, hidden corridors, and mirages that could get in the way. Like an ancient Wild West with bandits and outlaws at each turn.

Why does social media offer such fertile ground for manipulation? Because its very format encourages dependancy. I do no longer exaggerate when I say this; social media's algorithms and notifications are designed to preserve customers scrolling without surrender, supplying short doses of dopamine whilst notifications arrive, and capabilities that promote non-stop engagement - it's far like playing on your hobby; a person generally wins! Manipulators take benefit of its inherently addictive nature with the resource of manner of growing content cloth cloth that captures hobby however holds onto it.

Let's amplify upon this similarly: permit's maintain in mind echo chambers as an example. These are regions wherein all people holds comparable critiques, with any war of words being seemed down upon and regularly frowned upon.

Manipulators love echo chambers because of the fact as quickly as internal them it's miles like taking pictures fish in a barrel; you are supplied with limitless quantities of records that confirms what you already do not forget and makes you extra liable to manipulation. Be careful if your social feed will become one without understanding; it can occur subtly, almost with out be aware!

Let's turn our recognition in the path of social media's "cancel way of life," the predatory dog of social media. Manipulators use it to isolate and publicly disgrace people for perceived wrongs, developing an internet mob mentality. Not absolutely celebrities or influencers can come to be goals; virtually every person may be focused as any offense may also moreover purpose loss of employment and intellectual health deterioration - this doesn't imply responsibility need to no longer exist; as an opportunity it's far its disproportionate punishments with out a room for talk and redemption that makes this device used as a weapon of manipulation.

Wait a second! There's greater! Phishing scams, deep fakes and catfishing! I'm talking approximately intricate schemes designed to govern now not only your emotions, but moreover assault your wallet and private protection. A individual flirting with you on line is probably a person looking to convince you to cord coins their way or provide "too first rate to be actual" investment opportunities from a random Facebook pal who is in reality simply an attacker with a keyboard.

And allow's now not forget about the big gamers--governments and massive corporations--with their sizable assets for manipulation on an tremendous scale, the usage of social media to persuade public opinion, elections, and client conduct. Have you ever observed high quality topics trending mysteriously or classified ads appear tailor-made in particular for you? That is absolutely manipulation on an epic scale driven thru statistics analytics and intellectual profiling.

Awareness is the cornerstone of defense; whilst you apprehend their methods, you're extra prepared to defuse them with important wondering as your weapon of protection. Protect your non-public statistics like a beneficial treasure chest; be selective approximately who interacts with and shares what. Show warning in digital environments filled with trickery through cultivating healthy skepticism--that does not propose being an irritated man or woman, simply that you're cautious.

9.2 Phishing, Scams, and Online Fraud

Yup, this is the dark thing of the internet; wherein shady characters cover out from in the back of displays in region of in alleyways and are equipped to strike at the same time as a person becomes susceptible on line. Be warned - their recommendations ought to make even humans with thick pores and skin fall prey!

Phishing: Not your Uncle Joe's weekend hobby but a bootleg scheme in which scammers pose as valid establishments to scouse borrow sensitive information from patients. An email that appears exactly locate it irresistible got here from your bank with its brand, prompting you to log in because of some "suspicious pastime." However, its URL differs slightly; that is a lure and your login credentials captured for use later. However, not simply emails are targeted - textual content messages, pop-up commercials, smartphone calls also are powerful techniques of gathering login credentials.

Rule #1: Always double-test URL before giving out non-public records till it comes from its rightful proprietor!

Moving on to scams: Where have to one start? From pyramid schemes masquerading as business organization possibilities and faux lotteries purporting which you've obtained tens of heaps and lots amazing to call for you pay an alleged "small price," to unsolicited romantic hobbies forming emotional connections in advance than requesting cash - those scams prey upon emotions together with greed, love or fear and should be met with caution and skepticism as your best protection - ultimately you did now not input that lottery you in no way entered and likely aren't falling head over heels over that Instagram model who claims she/he/they need to truly give up!

But tech-savvy manipulators do now not save you there: we enter into the place of on-line fraud - that could take many paperwork, from faux stores that disappear when you make a buy to compromised social media debts marketing and advertising and marketing "incredible investment opportunities." Identity theft also exists in which thieves use your private statistics to open monetary organization money owed, exercise for credit score rating rating gambling playing cards, or document taxes beneath your call - it is all an excessive amount of!

How are you capable of stable yourself on-line? Begin through fortifying your digital citadel. Set strong passwords; "password123" may not do! Make use of -aspect authentication wherein viable and check economic enterprise statements regularly - if a few element appears amiss, file it straight away! Don't click on on hyperlinks or down load attachments from unknown sources and if a person sends unsolicited emails on the lookout for cash, personal facts or get proper of get admission to to for your pc, do not genuinely stroll away; run away much like the endure is even as you!

Well, I get it--the Internet can be intimidating. On one issue it offers consolation; on the opposite it could convey potential disaster. Don't strain too much despite the fact that--interest is 1/2 of the war acquired.

nine.Three How Algorithms Feed Manipulation

Yes, the ones unseen puppet masters pulling strings within the again of your social media feeds, are looking for outcomes, and purchasing guidelines on-line are actual and may have critical repercussions to your virtual existence. While you will probable take delivery of as actual with you are on pinnacle of things, clicking and scrolling freely, algorithms function unseen conductors orchestrating digital lifestyles; every so often this can be suitable (who does now not love customized playlists!?), at the same time as at times making you liable to manipulation.

Just what is an algorithm except? In its essence, an set of rules is clearly a fixed of recommendations or instructions followed via pc structures for you to carry out a assignment. When implemented to social structures like Facebook, Instagram, Google or YouTube however, algorithms end up nearly telepathic detectives: they look at your behavior thru tracking likes, stocks and comments in advance than making predictions on what content material material can also moreover moreover interest you next based totally on those measurements - but herein lies its downside - algorithms exist virtually to keep us engaged for as long as viable to be able to serve classified ads or manage reviews as a end result.

Imagine this: After searching one video approximately conspiracy theories for a laugh, abruptly your entire feed is filled with comparable posts - developing what's referred to as the "clear out bubble," restricting your worldview at the same time as growing vulnerability to manipulation and radicalization. Imagine being caught internal an echo chamber wherein all people is of the equal opinion along side your factor of view but no distinct voices emerge; filter out bubbles can speedy engulf you want an echo chamber, leaving best echoing voices obtainable that oppose.

But wait! Algorithms may also be weaponized for massive-scale manipulation. Have you heard of "deep fakes", hyper-practical fake films generated through manner of algorithms capable of making it seem that someone said or did some detail they never really said or did! Imagine their use for political manipulation or man or woman assassination!

Let's now not overlook the function that algorithms play in advert focused on. These sly lines of code understand you better than your mom does, making you an easy intention for particularly tailor-made advertising and marketing and advertising and marketing methods that take benefit of algorithms.

Chapter 9: Advanced Manipulation Techniques

10.1 Dark Triad: The Dangerous Trio

Hold on tight! We're going to research the Dark Triad--Narcissism, Machiavellianism, and Psychopathy--like an episode of a intellectual mystery. This risky trio does not embody random words thrown together without careful take a look at; those mental tendencies function the center of complicated manipulation techniques and traps. So buckle up; this superior playbook gives you with equipment for identifying masterminds of manipulation further to sidestepping their traps.

Narcissism is first on our list. Imagine someone who thinks the sun rises and devices at their whim. In their eyes, all people else in a movie is only a further. Narcissists commonly generally tend to very personal an inflated enjoy of self-importance that they may be keen on preserving. Like interest vampires, narcissists feed off admiration, compliments, and being on the center of interest; but do now not be fooled; their enchantment is as fleeting as fireworks. Dazzling then dissolving, leaving exceptional darkness in the lower back of it.

While they to start with appear charismatic, scratch under the surface and you can find out a loss of real problem for others. Ask your self: Does this man or woman take grievance like they were struck inside the face, avoid taking responsibility for their actions, and seem obsessed on their photograph, achievement and power? If those dispositions seem familiar to you, possibilities are true you've got recognized a narcissist.

Let's moreover delve into Machiavellianism, or puppeteer philosophy, named for Niccolo Machiavelli, an Italian Renaissance political advertising consultant renowned for writing The Prince, an in-intensity manual of political manipulation. Machiavellians view lifestyles like a grand venture board and are continuously shifting portions on it to benefit strategic benefits - in evaluation to an impulsive narcissist who can also make greater impulsive moves on it. Relationships for them come to be portions to transport for maximum strategic advantage with out regard for morality or values. At fine, their presence may be taken into consideration an inconvenience; at worst it's an try to manipulate. A high example can be someone gathering secrets like uncommon stamps for blackmailing talents later. If it looks like all they ever deliver once more is taken away in go lower back, possibly it is time to remember that you may be managing a grasp manipulator alternatively.

Psychopathy: the grand finale. Psychopaths represent the pinnacle predator inside the Dark Triad; while narcissists and Machiavellians might also additionally reputation on themselves and method, respectively, psychopaths lack simple emotional components like empathy or regret that make us people. They use this ability to carry out manipulative or poor acts with out being limited with the aid of moral codes that could typically keep others decrease returned. Not all sociopaths are serial killers or film villains; a few may be exceptionally functioning individuals of society who remain surely as risky. Their appeal also can appear harmless sufficient; however its lethal electricity may also resemble Venus flytrap's deadly hold over insects. Their impulsivity, whilst now and again making their movements unpredictable, additionally makes them hard to are anticipating.

So how do the ones traits combine? It's like an explosion of highbrow chaos. People who encompass factors of the Dark Triad make use of narcissism and charismatic conduct to draw people in, Machiavellian schemes for putting the scene for his or her plots, and psychopathy's bloodless, unforgiving middle to put in force manipulative techniques with none hint of guilt - developing an irreparable cycle of manipulative conduct that leaves destruction in its wake.

But do not be involved: being knowledgeable is energy! By understanding those trends and know-how their internal workings, you'll be better equipped to look through any deceit or misdirection and shield yourself through manner of setting company barriers, being cautious with non-public records, and trusting your intuition at the same time as some issue appears amiss. Consider this an in depth route in Advanced Manipulation Detection; hold intellectual shields up on the same time as the usage of your newfound records of The Dark Triad as armor towards human interactions that appear opaque or uncommon.

10.2 Advanced Gaslighting Techniques

Just even as you concept you had seen it all, along comes Advanced Gaslighting: the draw close beauty in manipulation techniques! No one asked for this enhance - but we want to dissect it for our very very personal sanity's sake. So let's dig in deep and discover each layer. Let's get down into it all now.

Basic gaslighting may additionally moreover seem harmless enough: changing history right here and growing doubt in reminiscences there. But advanced gaslighting is going similarly; it involves a couple of layers of mental manipulation woven so deeply into lifestyles that it will become nearly an paintings shape. A manipulator is going in addition than without a doubt changing fact; they craft an intricate maze in which each flip leads you similarly away from truth and nearer inside the direction of self-doubt, crucial you into an tricky labyrinth of lies so complicated it would make even Daedalus bewildered.

Before we dive in, allow's communicate about "Orchestrated Doubt." Imagine this: A gaslighter employs an army of flying monkeys (it definitely is highbrow jargon for minions in "The Wizard of Oz") to cause you to impeach yourself and your very private fact. They use buddies, circle of relatives and co-human beings as equipment of wrong records in their scheme that enhances its fake narrative, slowly the usage of doubt into your mind - the very human beings you normally turn to for truth assessments are surely a part of their play and contributing in the route of making doubt your sanity - making you query your self and questioning your very own sanity!

Next is "Strategic Forgetfulness." Imagine a person who virtually "forgets" some component that can positioned them at a disadvantage - for example in the event that they agreed to do some thing however did no longer have a look at thru? They need to efficaciously claim they have no reminiscence of that communication which locations all of the obligation onto you for "misremembering". Using this method masterfully turns you into an unwilling Sherlock Holmes!

Deniable Plausibility" is every other sneaky tactic utilized by gaslighters. Here, they supply incorrect information or hurtful remarks on the same time as veiling it with layers of ambiguity or humor, so if faced thru you they're able to play both "You misunderstood me" or "Can't you're taking a shaggy canine tale?" gambling playing cards to painting you as being oversensitive while in all likelihood pressured.

But that is no longer all! A specific function of Sanctified Gaslighting is whilst a manipulator makes use of non secular or moral ideals against you to gaslight you - as an example with the useful useful resource of saying they "remarkable choice" to save you from yourself ethical or non secular requirements that struggle with theirs, as a result undermining each perceptions of truth in addition to middle values similarly deepening manipulation's reach.

Yes, this will be overwhelming to take in. Perhaps you're wondering how you could shield in competition to such complicated manipulation. The key to powerful safety in competition to gaslighting lies with forensic-grade vigilance: write down statistics that can not be accessed with the useful resource of the gaslighter; keep your help community knowledgeable, if viable are seeking out advice from a intellectual fitness expert and bear in mind that gaslighting is based on you doubting yourself; as soon as that doubt goes a protracted manner from them their entire residence of playing cards collapses.

Chapter 10: Breaking Free And Recovery
eleven.1 Identifying the Exit Routes

Congratulations for installing there! At this factor, you will be asking, "Okay, so the sector is complete of manipulative techniques. What's my get away plan?" Excellent query! Identifying go out routes from manipulative situations calls for extra than definitely fleeing; as an alternative it consists of multi-layered procedures which can emerge as immensely freeing as quickly as understood.

Step one is "Self-Identification and Ownership". In order to interrupt free, you first need to find out what is trapping you. Although this might seem honest, now and again we get trapped so deeply internal ourselves that we don't even apprehend we're being managed - like being trapped in an limitless maze in which walls hold transferring! Before trying to crack someone else's mind video games, take inventory of yourself first: ask hard questions together with "What position have I achieved in this example?" and "Have I neglected caution signs and symptoms?" This step must not lead you toward self-blame but taking rate of your existence!

Once that step has been finished, glide onto the "Realization and Acknowledgment" stage. Here, it's far vital to understand your poisonous scenario and plan an exit method as fast as viable. No extra excuses; prevent telling yourself it's going to enhance thru trying more difficult or ready longer; take an motive have a observe all to be had records in advance than devising your go out method.

Now allow's flow into onto "Resources and Support Systems." This is your get away toolkit.

Communicate openly approximately your state of affairs to depended on human beings; easy eyes may also offer new belief. When suitable, are searching for advice from specialists - crook professionals, psychologists or some different experts pertinent on your case may provide precious assist right here;

accumulate evidence if critical and assemble your break out pod as a end result; the more stable it's miles constructed the extra its chance of a hit launching may be.

Hold on tight: the "Action Plan" is here! Outline unique steps you may take to get rid of your self from manipulation - whether or not or now not or now not which means quitting a mission, leaving an risky relationship or distancing yourself from an oppressor - despite the fact that there may be quick-time period downsides however popularity on prolonged-term rewards - your emotional and intellectual nicely-being must constantly come first!

"Post-Exit Recovery." Think you may stroll out and the whole thing will bypass decrease lower back to ordinary? Hollywood fantasies aside, lifestyles now not often seems that manner. In truth, but, the aftermath may be complex with the aid of emotional residue, keep in mind issues and monetary complications. Remember this degree can also provide opportunities for increase and restoration: pass into treatment or counseling lessons, interest on self-improvement sports activities sports or take that dream vacation! Your intention should be to rebuild more potent than earlier than.

eleven.2 Rebuilding Self-Esteem

Now is the time to have an excellent time! Breaking unfastened is truely momentous; now permit's popularity on rebuilding. Your self-esteem might also have visible better days; probable it has even languished somewhere deep inside its depths untouched for too prolonged. Now is the time to awaken it from its sleepy nation and convey it the the front and middle wherein it belongs; in any other case rebuilding will hold with out you even identifying.

Your first order of enterprise need to be an sincere assessment of your self. In order to construct an indestructible shallowness tower, it's far essential that you recognize wherein you stand with reference to inner beliefs and perceptions - in particular the way you view yourself currently; because of preceding manipulation, this belief might be barely skewed; much like taking walks via a hall entire of distorting mirrors at a carnival; the whole thing seems off stability. So eliminate the ones distorting lenses and recognition on who your actual self in reality is.

After this step is "Mental Script Flipping." Simply placed, this exercising consists of flipping your script in terms of what it says about who you're in your head. If the cutting-edge narrative tells us that we're pushovers or unworthy, it is time to switch out those narratives with ones collectively with: "I am deserving," "I am sturdy," and "I am empowered". No want for wishful questioning here-- this cognitive restructuring exercising gadgets the level for first-rate intellectual shift from static kingdom to dynamic increase, on the identical time as giving ourselves device that build upon themselves over time! Neuroscience backs this approach with the useful resource of the usage of presenting us all with frameworks essential for change over the years!

Now allow's delve into "Affirmative Actions." Not in fact affirmations, however movements that verify your well well worth. Think of this due to the fact the tangible implementation of your highbrow scripts: what sports or accomplishments make you enjoy like one million greenbacks? Focus on them as activities you can include into your normal lifestyles: be it playing sports activities sports efficiently, mastering culinary dishes from around the world or earning praise at paintings - those all assist collect on and solidify the modern-day narrative approximately you which you're developing for yourself.

Just to make clear, "Squad Goals" refers to your cheerleading squad at the same time as rebuilding your vanity. Social assist is not most effective a revel in-appropriate cliche; studies suggests it improves intellectual health. Surround yourself with people who apprehend you for who you truly are and admire who you are with all your flaws; percentage fears and triumphs and setbacks with them for validation, and let their help characteristic wind under your wings; it's far like having an emotional protection net geared up simply in case desired - comforting understanding it exists surely in case!

Micro-Victories and Cumulative Success. Instead of striving to achieve unbelievable heights from day one, recognition on small victories which is probably ability and assemble upon them until they devise a feel of success - this may help bolster fragile conceitedness by means of the use of supplying evidence of your abilties, competence and fundamental awesomeness - in the long run flooding your thoughts with worthwhile neurochemicals like dopamine and serotonin that make you experience outstanding!

Self-Compassion and Kindness." Rebuilding arrogance might not come without issue; its adventure may be marked with bumps, potholes and coffee roadblocks. When handling setbacks - that you always will - view them as opportunities to have a look at yourself in preference to screw ups that outline who you are as a person. Realize that setbacks are a part of being human - no one's best 100% of the time!

Rebuilding your self-esteem is like renovating an vintage house; it takes time, artwork, and emotional attempt. Each nail you hammer in, every plank you region strengthens you - making you stronger toward manipulation in destiny encounters; every step towards strengthening and fortifying yourself counts as development in the path of prevailing this struggle in its entirety.

eleven.Three Emotional Detox: Cleansing the Mind

Congratulations on making it this a ways in your recuperation adventure from manipulation. Now it's time to appearance in advance, but. Before sprinting within the route of the stop line, we should cope with a few thing vital: emotional detox. No, that is no modern day nicely-being fashion; instead it includes all-out purifying of mental space which may additionally furthermore however consist of poisonous remnants of manipulation.

Recognize and Acknowledge" is the preliminary section on this undertaking; reflect onconsideration on it like reconnaissance of an emotional battlefield. There may be residual highbrow debris left from past evaluations along with anger, disappointment or self-doubt that need to first be diagnosed earlier than doing some aspect about them. Don't deal with this like passive statement - take inventory of all emotions encountered at the same time as actively acknowledging them to reduce the electricity of monsters under bed!

So permit's transition into segment - Emotional Alchemy." In essence, you're going to become a intellectual alchemist and transform those poisonous emotions into a few element useful - like anger as an example! Channel that burning anger into extraordinary alternate indoors your life through becoming a member of a fitness regime, taking up a hobby, or developing productivity at art work - like pouring those toxic feelings thru a crucible with warmness flames earlier than boiling away all their nasty element-consequences and casting off into 24-karat gold.

Take a destroy from all your thoughts, issues and fears and actually be gift inside the 2d - I'm talking whole-on mindfulness meditation here - sitting nonetheless, respiration deeply and permitting any stray mind that arise to skip without attaching too tightly to them. Science backs it up: mindfulness can reduce strain, decrease tension tiers and decorate intellectual readability - the intellectual identical of strength washing your deck!

Now it is time for Cognitive Decontamination." Cognitive Behavioral Therapy (CBT), regularly diagnosed via its acronym, Cognitive Behavior Analysis or CBA is used by psychologists and therapists as a powerful manner to understand dangerous idea patterns or distortions that have crept into your psyche, collectively with catastrophizing or wearing out black-and-white thinking. CBT strategies will help find out poisonous idea patterns, challenge them, and replace them with greater rational, balanced thoughts - like changing vintage pipes in your home with cutting-edge outstanding pipes - out with antique, in comes new.

Once we're nicely underway with this method, permit's shift gears and explore "Emotional Circuit Training." Emotional resilience is much like bodily strength: It goals regular carrying occasions definitely as a good deal for development. So workout emotional coping techniques which include journaling, artwork treatment or dance as strategies of strengthening emotional muscle mass regularly and make this part of your every day everyday.

Now that our operation has come to a near, I need you to hold one final degree in thoughts: "Relapse Prevention and Maintenance." A detox isn't some thing that takes area as fast as and is then forgotten about for some other 12 months; emotional landscapes need regular preservation too! Set intellectual checkpoints--possibly with yourself monthly self-assessments or discussions with a therapist or depended on buddy--to make sure you are staying on course.

Emotional detox is not a one-day affair; rather, it calls for complete and multifaceted paintings on multiple fronts to achieve real transformation. Think of it like this: emotional detox is a marathon run in place of a dash race that guarantees entire rejuvenation of the mind, reset of emotional compass and constructing of a new, resilient self. In essence, you are clearing out emotional particles in your emotional junk drawer, organizing its contents after which filling once more up simplest with those equipment which offer nourishment in your adventure ahead.

eleven.Four Benefits of Support Networks

Like superhero films, our maximum essential protagonist commonly goals guide from his or her corporation - collectively with the Avengers, X-Men or maybe Harry, Ron and Hermione in Harry Potter! While our heroes can be robust on their private, their strength amplifies drastically while joined with others - this same precept holds real for your journey faraway from manipulation and inside the course of right restoration. You can also have achieved hard art work in emotional detox, but underestimated how essential an established useful resource community may be in helping you on this course - taking "It takes a village" to coronary coronary coronary heart!

Start off this communication through thinking about "Community as Emotional Anchor." Having pals and family round can serve more than in truth as records noise; the ones relationships feature your anchor to fact at the same time as a person else has been messing collectively with your perceptions for a while. Imagine your self crusing in tough waters; your network serves as each lighthouse and harbor concurrently while someone manipulates your fact into wondering your sanity; gaslighting turns into loads more difficult to tug off whilst there may be someone putting beforehand your research and perceptions.

Oh and now permit's dive into "Therapeutic Friendships." As with some aspect in lifestyles, no longer all friendships offer equal emotional help. While some buddies is probably exquisite for a wild night out, others can truely provide useful emotional manual during instances of want. Such relationships move deeper than simply casual hold close-out periods: they provide healing remedy like no tremendous relationship can. Just as vegetation require vitamins to develop well, severa friends offer emotional sustenance that might range from validation, recommendation or without a doubt listening ears - famend each one because it comes and nurture those relationships like an overgrown lawn!

But being part of a help network does now not clearly encompass taking; it moreover involves giving. That's why know-how the dynamics of a balanced assist network is so critical. Imagine stacking blocks on one element at the same time as great setting some on others; ultimately that tower may disintegrate below its very very very own weight, prompting emotional meltdown. Your useful resource community should replicate this idea: no longer sincerely leaning on others for assist; you need to moreover provide yourself assist as part of its fabric. When helping others you not at once remind your self of your very private skills.

Chapter 11: Exploring The Essence Of Dark Psychology

Modifications for a More Fluid Reading

1. Vocabulary and Language Use:

Consider simplifying complicated terms and the usage of greater straightforward language to increase accessibility for a broader goal marketplace.

Avoid overly complex sentence systems; hold sentences concise and centered.

2. Narrative Flow:

Ensure transitions amongst subjects and sections are easy, guiding the reader seamlessly from one concept to some other.

Introduce actual-lifestyles examples or memories earlier to demonstrate requirements and engage readers.

3. Engagement:

Integrate questions or direct addresses to the reader to make the narrative extra interactive and appealing.

Use more storytelling elements to deliver precis concepts to existence.

What Dark Psychology Entails

Exploring the depths of human behavior and the difficult psychology that underlies our movements and reactions is corresponding to diving into an enigmatic ocean, rife with mysteries, wonders, and every now and then, sinister factors that lurk in the shadowy depths. One such element, each charming and haunting, is dark psychology. This term encompasses those components of human cognition and behavior marked by manipulation, exploitation, and deception. In the tough ballet of human interactions, dark psychology is the choreography of unseen strings, the silent puppeteer maneuvering behind the scenes.

In our every day lives, we placed on countless masks, assume severa roles, and navigate through an problematic dance of social norms, expectations, and mutual affects. In this complicated dance, dark psychology emerges due to the reality the unseen force, the silent whisper that sways, manipulates, and sometimes dictates our moves, reactions, and interactions. It is a pressure both diffused and powerful, quiet but devastating. It is not manifested through overt coercion or seen pressure but operates through whispers, hints, and the ethereal, but profound, strokes of invisible affects.

Dark psychology is not a global of black and white but is living in the sun shades of grey that shade human interactions. Every conduct, every motion, every response on this realm is laced with unspoken intentions, hidden reasons, and unseen

influences. Each word spoken, every gesture made, isn't always a spontaneous act but a calculated flow into, every syllable and motion imbued with layers of meanings, intentions, and capability affects. Our information of darkish psychology unravels a silent however prevailing force, wherein strength dynamics aren't asserted however insinuated, wherein manage isn't enforced however silently instilled. Every alternate, every communication, each interaction isn't a mere transaction but a complicated dance of intellectual nuances, orchestrated to serve, assert, and every now and then manage the latent, regularly unacknowledged, electricity equations that underlie human relationships.

Yet, to label darkish psychology as an inherent evil or malevolent stress can be an oversimplification. It is not a weapon but a device, its moral and ethical ramifications bobbing up not from its life but its utility. Every person, irrespective of their overt behaviors, harbors the seeds of dark mental influences. These seeds, even though regularly dormant, are first-rate, their silent whispers steerage our behaviors, choices, and lifestyles options.

In the theater of lifestyles, we are each the puppeteers and the puppets, the influencers and the stimulated. Our actions are every self preserving and manipulated, our picks both self-derived and externally stimulated. This paradox isn't a contradiction however a sworn assertion to the complex, multifaceted nature of human psychology.

As we delve deeper into this captivating but unsettling global, we unveil the hidden scripts that underlie human behaviors. Each phrase, every motion, each reaction is a tale, a story scripted now not without a doubt with the aid of aware intentions but with the aid of unseen, frequently unacknowledged, mental forces. In the arena of darkish psychology, perceptions are not reflections of an goal fact however structures, cautiously crafted through manipulations diffused but profound.

In our journey of exploration, we aren't passive observers but active human beings. Every step we take, every revelation we unveil, isn't always a passive discovery however an energetic engagement with the hidden dimensions of human psychology. Every truth unearthed, each thriller unraveled, is a step inside the path of empowerment, an enhancement of our intellectual autonomy.

In the intricacies of dark psychology, we discover not truely the silent puppeteers of manipulation and manipulate however additionally the keys to our chains, the gear to reclaim our psychological freedom. Every revelation, every notion, isn't a step into the darkness however a stride in the course of mild, a journey from

manipulated puppetry to empowered autonomy.

The essence of darkish psychology isn't rooted in overt manipulations however diffused impacts. It isn't always the area of black magic or express coercion however a realm of silent whispers, unseen strings, and invisible palms that steer the ship of human behaviors thru the turbulent waters of social, intellectual, and interpersonal dynamics.

In this worldwide, manipulations aren't enacted but insinuated, influences now not enforced however instilled. The puppeteer does no longer wield a seen hand but operates from the shadows, his strings woven via the problematic tapestry of human feelings, cognitions, and behaviors.

To apprehend dark psychology is to embark on a journey not of discovery however of revelation, not of mastering however of unlearning. It is a way of peeling away the layers of overt behaviors to unveil the hidden scripts, the silent narratives that script the story of human interactions. It is a dance of displaying, a ballet of revelation, in which every step, each flip, unveils no longer clearly the hidden dimensions of human interactions but the unseen corridors of our non-public psyche.

As we delve deeper into this enigmatic global, each revelation is a reflect, reflecting no longer just the hidden faces of our fellow beings however our hid selves. We are not certainly the explorers of this enigmatic global however moreover its population, not genuinely the seekers of its hidden truths however moreover the bearers of its hid secrets and techniques and techniques.

Every revelation, every perception, each unveiled fact is a step inside the direction of self-discovery, a journey within the course of self-revelation. In the silent corridors of dark psychology, we discover now not honestly the hidden puppeteers of out of doors impacts but the hid puppetry of our inner international.

In this adventure of revelation and discovery, darkness is not an enemy but an high-quality buddy, silence now not a void but a tale, and invisibility not a loss of lifestyles but a testimony to the profound overall performance of the unseen.

Our exploration of dark psychology isn't a passive remark but an energetic engagement.

We are not mere spectators of this hard dance however active dancers, our steps, turns, and maneuvers each scripted and self sustaining, stimulated and influential, manipulated and manipulative.

In the enigmatic dance of darkish psychology, we are each the puppeteers and the puppets, the dancers and the dance, the observers and the located. Every step is each a revelation and a mystery, each turn each an unveiling and a concealment, every notion each a discovery and an enigma.

As we immerse ourselves on this intricate dance, every revelation is an empowerment, every unveiled truth a step within the path of autonomy, and every unmasked mystery a stride inside the direction of freedom. In the silent however eloquent narrative of dark psychology, we are not genuinely the readers of its hidden scripts however the authors of our unveiled memories, not sincerely the observers of its silent dance but the choreographers of our empowered steps.

In this dance of darkness and mild, manipulation and autonomy, impact and empowerment, we are not passive puppets but energetic puppeteers, our strings each wielded and wielded, our dances every scripted and independent, our

narratives each narrated and narrating. In the enigmatic worldwide of darkish psychology, we are every the dance and the dancers, the puppet and the puppeteer, the narrative and the narrators.

The adventure into the geographical regions of darkish psychology is not a descent into darkness however an ascent into mild, now not a passage into manipulation however a stride into autonomy, now not an immersion into silence but a dance to the eloquent tunes of unstated narratives and hidden scripts. Every revelation is a step towards mild, each unveiled reality a stride toward freedom, and every unmasked manipulation a dance closer to autonomy.

An Insight into Narcissism, Machiavellianism, and Psychopathy

The silent symphony of the human psyche, a tale every profound and enigmatic, is residing in a dance of hid forces. Therein, amidst the everyday harmonies of human connections and interactions, lies the darker traces of human psychology. To challenge into those hidden geographical regions is to unmask the sinister trio – Narcissism, Machiavellianism, and Psychopathy – the enigmatic factors that solid a silent shadow over the lustrous panorama of the human soul. As we adventure through the twilight zones of those intellectual enigmas, we unveil a tale, eerie however charming, of the concealed corridors of human motivations and intentions.

Narcissism: The Icarian Dance

Narcissism, much like the mythic Icarus, is a dance of the self, a ballet in which the 'I' is both the dancer and the dance. The narcissist lives in a worldwide mirrored via the self, wherein reflections are not of the arena however of the soul, refracted thru the prisms of self-adulation. Every admiration is a sonnet, each reward a symphony, but in this orchestra of adulations, lies the silent pressure of an insidious solitude.

In the mind of the narcissist, others are however silhouettes, solar sun shades without substance, echoing the hollow symphony of the self. Relationships, no matter the truth that adorned through the facade of

intimacy, are silent soliloquies, monologues masquerading as dialogues. The narcissist, entranced via the melody of self-admiration, is unaware of the harmonies of reciprocity, deaf to the symphonies of mutual admiration.

Yet, amidst the radiant glow of self-love lies the haunting shadow of an intrinsic loss of self assurance. The narcissist, similar to Icarus, is all the time in flight, hovering the skies of self-adulation, but haunted through way of using the silent spectre of a fall, an ominous plunge into the abyss of self-doubt, self-loathing.

Every praise is a wing, but each silence a silent stress, an ominous prelude to the approaching plunge.

Machiavellianism: The Silent Puppeteer

In the eerie silence of manipulations concealed, echoes the haunting melody of Machiavellianism. Here lies the puppeteer, his strings woven through the silent corridors of human psyche, his puppetry a dance of shadows, eerie but profound. The Machiavellian mind is an enigma, a riddle wrapped in mystery, an equation unsolved.

Power, to the Machiavellian, isn't a ownership however a play, no longer a treasure however a dance. Relationships aren't connections but conquests, now not bonds but battles. Every interplay is a way, each connection a conquest, each affection a weapon, wielded with the sinister splendor of a puppeteer, silent but effective.

Chapter 12: Deciphering The Art Of Manipulation

Grasping the Concept of Manipulation

In the elaborate net of human interactions, few elements are as top notch and pervasive as manipulation. This pressure, diffused however commanding, operates within the backdrop of our day by day communications, shaping choices, guiding emotions, and, at times, redirecting the path of lives. Whether it's miles the seemingly innocent persuasion of a little one wanting a similarly cookie earlier than dinner or the calculated techniques of a pro negotiator, manipulation exhibits its manner into many components of our lifestyles. But what precisely is manipulation, and the way does it wield such have an impact on over us? Manipulation, in essence, is the act of influencing someone's beliefs, feelings, intentions, or behaviors in a covert way. It's not generally malicious. In reality, it frequently is dwelling in grey areas, making it hard to categorize definitively as perfect or terrible. Its nature is rooted deeply in reason. Just as water can quench thirst or drown, manipulation can empower or entrap, counting on how it is hired. Dive deeper into the world of manipulation, and you could find it's greater than mere deceit or lying. It's a complicated art work that hinges on expertise human psychology, feelings, and vulnerabilities. To illustrate, do not forget a hobby of chess. On the surface, it's approximately transferring portions at some point of a board. But at its coronary coronary coronary heart, chess is a recreation of method, anticipation, and influencing your opponent's moves. Similarly, manipulation is ready orchestrating conditions, predicting reactions, and guiding effects.

Flattery serves as an illustrative instance. A right compliment can brighten someone's day, boosting their self guarantee. However, at the same time as used as a device via a manipulator, flattery becomes a way to an prevent. An insincere praise might be employed to decrease a person's defenses, making them more susceptible to idea. Suddenly, the line between real appreciation and strategic maneuvering blurs, and the person, swayed via the use of the enchantment of flattery, may additionally act in techniques they otherwise could not. Emotion, in fact, is the best forex in a manipulator's arsenal. By tapping into the notable reservoir of human feelings—be it love, fear, envy, or delight—a manipulator can steer an man or woman's movements and alternatives.

Think approximately the last time you made an impulsive buy due to the truth a shop clerk instilled a experience of urgency or a fear of lacking out. "This offer may not final!" or "Only a few left in stock!" Such statements motive to bypass logical thinking, urging immediately motion. And greater often than now not, they be triumphant. Yet, now not all manipulation stems from an area of deceit or self-gain. Consider the area of remedy. Therapists regularly appoint manipulative techniques, subtly guiding conversations, asking pointed questions, or the usage of particular techniques to help patients confront and paintings thru their problems. In this context, manipulation aids in restoration and boom.

Similarly, leaders—be it in organizations, communities, or international places—often must employ manipulative strategies for the greater right. Guiding a set thru a tough phase, rallying humans in the back of a cause, or navigating excessive-stakes negotiations might probably require a leader to manipulate situations, facts flow, or even emotions to a degree. Here, manipulation seeks to attain a collective purpose, frequently reaping benefits the bigger company.

However, the double-edged nature of manipulation will become starkly evident even as it falls into the incorrect hands. Swindlers, con artists, and people with malicious cause can wield it to make the most, deceive, and harm. Here, manipulation isn't pretty a good deal guiding selections—it's far about manipulate. Such people or entities are attempting to find to dominate, reducing others to mere puppets of their grand scheme.

So, how does one navigate a international rife with manipulation? Awareness is the primary line of protection. Recognizing while and how one is being manipulated is important. It's approximately facts the distinction amongst being endorsed and being managed. It's approximately discerning actual purpose from deceit. Knowledge of the severa manipulative procedures—how they will be hired, their signs, and their consequences—empowers individuals to make informed picks.

Furthermore, introspection performs a pivotal characteristic. Understanding one's vulnerabilities, emotional triggers, and biases may need to make it more difficult for manipulators to take advantage of them. If

you understand that you have a penchant for succumbing to flattery or a worry of lacking out, spotting on the same time as those are becoming applied in opposition to you becomes less hard.

On a broader scale, fostering open communique channels, in which intentions and motives are apparent, can mitigate the consequences of manipulation. Encouraging environments wherein questions are welcomed, alternatives are collectively made, and hidden agendas don't have any place can considerably

reduce the scope for manipulation.

In end, manipulation, with its outstanding spectrum beginning from harmless persuasion to malicious control, is an inherent part of human interactions. Its presence is straightforward, however its outcomes, each superb and bad, hinge in big part on purpose. As we strive to manual real lives, knowledge, recognizing, and responsibly the use of manipulation becomes paramount. After all, in the dance of human interactions, it's no longer approximately averting manipulation however analyzing the art work of the use of it ethically and defensive in opposition to its misuse.

Unpacking the Power Play in Manipulation

The Theater of Human Interactions

In every exchange, be it a casual verbal exchange amongst friends or a immoderate-stakes commercial organisation negotiation, there exists a diffused dance of electricity dynamics. This unspoken ballet choreographs who leads, who follows, and who in the end achieves their desired very last effects. The essence of this strength play is maximum palpably felt inside the art of manipulation.

When we speak of manipulation, it regularly inspires a horrible sentiment. The word conjures pics of puppet masters pulling strings, of diffused deceit weaving its way through take transport of as authentic with. But as with each system, its effect and ethical weight are contingent upon the purpose and execution of the wielder. And to really apprehend it, we ought to dissect the energy systems that underscore its mechanisms.

The Dynamics of Power

Power, within the context of human interactions, isn't really approximately bodily energy or authoritative dominance. It is the potential to steer the selection-making tactics, moves, or emotional states of others. This capability can stem from severa property: expertise, air of mystery, socioeconomic reputation, or sheer force of character, to name some. It is fluid, regularly moving from one celebration to a few different inside the route of an interaction.

Manipulation is largely the tactical use of this strength to influence outcomes. But why do humans are seeking out to govern? At its center, the incentive regularly boils all of the way all of the manner all the way down to fear or choice—fear of loss, of inadequacy, of being unnoticed; or the selection for more— more manage, extra validation, extra protection.

The Elements of Effective Manipulation

For manipulation to be powerful, it should be discreet. It's the moderate tug, not the forceful push, that regularly achieves the intended final consequences. Here, statistics is paramount. A expert manipulator is adept at analyzing situations, discerning vulnerabilities, and crafting strategies that resonate with the individual psyche.

Empathy, the Double-Edged Sword: At first glance, empathy could likely seem contrary to manipulation. After all, isn't empathy approximately knowledge and sharing a few different's feelings? Precisely. It's this deep knowledge that can be used to craft resonating messages, to faucet into insecurities, aspirations, or desires. In the hands of a manipulator, empathy becomes the map to navigate the human psyche.

The Art of Persuasive Communication: This is ready more than certainly eloquence. It's approximately framing, tone, timing, and context. It's the reassuring contact at the shoulder, the understanding appearance, the hint of a shared thriller. Manipulators excel at crafting narratives that create a experience of urgency, scarcity, or exclusivity, urging their intention inside the direction of a particular direction of motion.

Emotional Resonance: The maximum effective of manipulative techniques comprise emotional engagement. Whether it is nostalgia, a shared enemy, or a not unusual dream, if a manipulator could have interaction you emotionally, logical defenses regularly disintegrate. An emotionally charged individual is greater at risk of recommendations, making them an much less complicated purpose.

The Dangers of Misused Power

But, as with any topics effective, there can be a darkish element. Misused, manipulation can result in exploitation, emotional trauma, and a breakdown of believe. This misuse is particularly egregious in intimate settings, wherein accept as true with need to be the foundation.

Consider relationships, familial or romantic, in which one companion continuously manipulates the alternative. Over time, this erodes be given as actual with, breeds resentment, and can lead to excessive mental repercussions. The victim, often oblivious to the manipulation, can also internalize feelings of inadequacy or guilt. They may additionally additionally moreover start to question their

well worth, their judgment, their very
identity.

Chapter 13: The World Of Mind Control

In the quiet corners of bustling towns, in the depths of the digital global, and even within the intimate regions of our non-public relationships, there lies a realm that worrying conditions our know-how of human behavior. This realm, interesting but menacing, is the place of thoughts control. As vintage as human interplay however as cutting-edge as the brand new technology, thoughts manage weaves a complex tapestry that entangles emotion, psychology, and power dynamics.

Delve into any historical civilization, from the potent Roman Empire to the an extended way-reaching dynasties of China, and you may find out reminiscences of emperors, philosophers, and commoners grappling with the concept of influencing some other's thoughts. Whether it modified into through eloquent rhetoric, non secular dogmas, or perhaps the melodies of historic bards, there has usually been a quest to sway, to steer, and to control. In those historic narratives, the interaction among unfastened will and outside effect have become a valuable topic, a philosophical puzzle that challenged incredible minds.

Fast ahead to these days, and the scene is each acquainted and strikingly special. The ranges have shifted from grand coliseums to digital systems, from hushed palace corridors to organisation boardrooms. Yet, the underlying human desire stays unchanged: to apprehend the workings of the mind and, in a few instances, to manipulate it.

But why does this preference exist? At its center, the pursuit of mind manipulate is a quest for energy. To manage one's surroundings, to are anticipating responses, to navigate the complexities of societal hierarchies, all boil down to the age-vintage electricity dynamics. With strength comes safety, manage, and supremacy. In the enterprise jungles of the twenty first century or the power corridors of contemporary-day politics, this information of the human psyche may be the difference among dominance and obsolescence.

Yet, the area of mind manipulate is not just about domination. It's a dance, once in a while diffused, every now and then overt, some of the influencer and the stimulated. There are people who wield this statistics with care, the usage of it to encourage, encourage, and uplift. Teachers, leaders, and mentors who harness the know-how of human behavior to foster increase, tapping into aspirations and desires. On the other give up of the spectrum, however, are folks who misuse this knowledge, important to memories of manipulation, exploitation, and loss of self-employer corporation.

This financial catastrophe will adventure via this complicated international, losing mild on the evolution of mind manage theories and unveiling the techniques which have been honed over millennia. Through poignant case research, the narrative will offer a replicate to society, reflecting each its luminous aspirations and its shadowy recesses.

Tracing the Evolution of Mind Control Theories

In the huge tapestry of human information, few threads were as compelling and debatable because the theories surrounding mind manipulate. From the primary murmurings of oracles in ancient temples to the meticulous research of new neuroscientists, human beings have prolonged been worried with the ability to influence every other's thoughts, ideals, or behaviors. This pull isn't always merely approximately electricity or dominance; it is woven into our essential pressure to connect, recognize, and form our shared reality. Historically, our ancestors believed inside the supernatural strength of phrases. They reputable and feared the charismatic leaders, shamans, and mystics who want to seemingly bend the choice of the masses through not some thing greater than speech. In ancient

Greece, for instance, rhetoric—the paintings of persuasive speaking—became a subject of incredible look at.

Thinkers like Aristotle meticulously dissected how language might be wielded to encourage, seduce, or mislead. But it modified into within the 20th century, in competition to a backdrop of global conflicts and transferring societal norms, that the have a take a look at of thoughts manipulate superior from a combination of myth, superstition, and anecdotal evidence into a extra rigorous scientific difficulty. The horrors of World War II, specially the upward push of propaganda machines and evaluations of brainwashing in prisoner-of-conflict camps, gave impetus to Western powers, especially america, to dig deeper into the mechanics of the human mind.

The Cold War generation, fraught with its tensions, introduced the overall public to the time period "brainwashing." This phrase conjured pix of vacant-eyed soldiers, spies betraying their nations after being "grew to turn out to be," and civilians espousing ideologies alien to their upbringing—all allegedly the quit result of insidious strategies employed with the beneficial aid of the enemy. The idea that someone's deeply held beliefs and recollections can be overwritten or manipulated become every captivating and terrifying. However, due to the fact the decades superior, studies commenced out to debunk many famous myths about brainwashing. Scientists got here to recognize that at the equal time as it's feasible to exert widespread have an impact on on a person, in particular underneath situations of severe duress, the perception of absolutely overwriting someone's character or ideals is a long way-fetched. Human minds are remarkably resilient, and at the same time as they can be bent, they may be not resultseasily broken. Neurological research within the latter part of the twentieth century commenced to offer some insights into why and the way human beings are susceptible to influence. Our brains are pressured for connection, and we've got superior to live interior groups. This social nature approach we're attuned to the behaviors, ideals, and critiques of these spherical us. In many procedures, our brains are primed for conformity because of the fact, traditionally, going toward the institution may also want to have dire results.

In the place of psychology, research delved into phenomena like groupthink, conformity, and obedience to authority. One of the most well-known—or notorious—of these end up the Stanford jail experiment led with the aid of manner of Philip Zimbardo, which showcased how resultseasily people might also want to slip into roles of oppressors or the oppressed, given the right environment. While it raised severa moral troubles, the test showed the profound impact of situational and systemic forces on man or woman behavior.

As the twenty first century dawned, era added a new size to our know-how of mind manage. The upward thrust of the net and, later, social media systems revolutionized verbal exchange. These gear, designed initially to hold humans nearer, moreover have turn out to be wonderful devices of have an effect on. Algorithms that track customers' behaviors and options ought to micro-intention human beings with information tailor-made to their biases, developing echo chambers and reinforcing pre-modern-day beliefs.

But it wasn't simply the digital realm that provided insights. As neuroscientists obtained get right of entry to to greater modern day equipment like practical MRI scans, they commenced out to "see" the brain in motion. This opened doorways to information how one-of-a-type stimuli—whether or now not terms, pictures, or evaluations—should set off or suppress severa areas of the mind associated with emotion, choice-making, or maybe our experience of self.

The adventure of statistics mind control is a long manner from over. Every year, researchers unearth greater nuances about how our brains paintings, how we system statistics, and the way we can be brought on. But what is easy is that thoughts manipulate, in its maximum dramatic depiction, stays greater the stuff of technological understanding fiction than fact. Instead, the subtle, normal influences of circle of relatives, society, life-style, and now, virtual algorithms, shape our perceptions and movements.

As we replicate upon this evolution, it's important to broadly identified our inherent vulnerability and to apprehend the forces that sway us. Doing so equips us to navigate our contemporary worldwide with more discernment, making sure that whilst we may be inspired, we are in no manner sincerely controlled. This attention, coupled with a dedication to essential thinking and self-reflected photograph, remains our satisfactory safety in a global brimming with messages vying for our hobby and allegiance.

Unveiling Brainwashing Techniques

In the widespread landscape of dark psychology, few strategies evoke as a whole lot worry, fascination, and delusion as brainwashing. Often visualized as a form of severe manipulation, brainwashing has been depicted in numerous cultural settings from Cold War espionage memories to modern-day films. This financial catastrophe will delve into expertise brainwashing, no longer as a legendary tool however as a concrete, intellectual exercising.

Brainwashing, in its best terms, refers back to the methodical use of techniques and strategies to modify a person's beliefs, attitudes, and behaviors without their consent or interest. This transformation isn't always moderate; it's far about radical shifts that could bring about people acting contrary to their previous ideals or pastimes.

Origins of the Term

The time period "brainwashing" become first coined in the Nineteen Fifties all through the Korean War, even as tales of captured American squaddies renouncing their area of starting place and praising their captors' ideologies started making headlines. Journalists, looking to draw close the character of those sudden turn of sports, depended on a translation of the Chinese term "xǐnǎo", which actually interprets to "wash mind". While the concept of manipulating minds has existed for hundreds of years, the time period "brainwashing" crystallized it inside the current era.

The Three-Stage Process of Brainwashing

Historically and academically, brainwashing can be distilled proper proper right into a three-diploma system: breaking down the self, introducing the opportunity of salvation, and rebuilding of the self. Breaking Down the Self: This initial phase is all approximately destabilizing someone's experience of identification and expertise of the arena. This is executed through a combination of excessive highbrow pressure and bodily harm, if now not outright torture. Sleep deprivation, isolation from acquainted surroundings and cherished ones, and constant wondering or verbal abuse are just a few methods employed. The intention? To make the person doubt the whole lot they formerly held pricey, from their non-public beliefs to their statistics of truth. Introducing the Possibility of Salvation: Just on the same time because the character is at their maximum willing, having been stripped of their identity and ideals, the brainwasher gives an answer: salvation. But this isn't salvation in a religious enjoy, although it can take that shape. It's about providing a new ideology or notion system as the most effective route to redemption, comfort, or survival. Rebuilding of the Self: The very last degree sees the character often starting to adopt the today's beliefs as their very personal, relinquishing their vintage self completely. By now, the man or woman is regularly in a rustic of such intellectual fragility that they'll be determined for any form of shape or meaning, making them greater vulnerable to wholeheartedly embracing what is provided.

Real-World Examples

To bring this out of the world of idea, endure in mind historic instances similar to the Cultural Revolution in China. This movement observed tens of heaps and thousands of humans, such as intellectuals and college university students, being despatched to re-training camps. The giant "re-schooling" techniques they underwent bore all of the hallmarks of brainwashing, from public humiliation and forced confessions to the adoption of a modern-day, kingdom-authorized set of ideals. Another putting example is the notorious Jonestown Massacre, wherein over 900 fanatics of cult leader Jim Jones died in a mass homicide-suicide event. Jones used brainwashing strategies, from isolation and bodily punishment to steady publicity to his teachings, making his lovers recollect that their handiest salvation lay in following his instructions, even to the amount of taking their private lives. The Science Behind Brainwashing While the idea of brainwashing can also appear nearly supernatural, there can be actual technological know-how inside the again of it. It is primarily based closely on our mind's plasticity—the ability to exchange and adapt. When subjected to immoderate strain or trauma, the mind releases a flurry of hormones. In small doses, the ones are protective. But within the sustained, immoderate amounts experienced all through brainwashing, they can motive harm, impairing our capability to anticipate considerably and making us extra impressionable. The ordinary stress forces the mind right into a hyper-adaptive mode, making it more

vulnerable to accepting new data without the usual

vital analysis.

Moreover, human beings are inherently social beings, and isolation could have profound mental consequences. We rely on social remarks to inform plenty of our ideals and actions. By reducing a person off from acquainted social comments and converting it with a novel, frequently distorted supply of statistics, you may drastically modify their worldview.

Overcoming Brainwashing

Undoing brainwashing isn't always a honest challenge. It frequently requires the same widespread, prolonged approach however in opposite. De-radicalization applications, as an example, hire extended counseling, publicity to opportunity viewpoints, and the rebuilding of the man or woman's real identification. For the ones mother and father not right away affected but looking to defend in the direction of such manipulation, knowledge remains our maximum top notch weapon. Understanding the mechanics of brainwashing, spotting its symptoms and signs, and having a strong feel of self can provide some diploma of protection. In end, brainwashing is a effective reminder of the human thoughts's fragility. But it moreover underscores our resilience and the great functionality to rebuild even after present process severe mental trauma. As we navigate our present day global, brimming with a deluge of facts and attempts at impact, might also we be ever vigilant, severely studying the information we consume, and continuously staying real to ourselves.

Undoing brainwashing is not a sincere mission. It often requires the identical intensive, prolonged method but in contrary. De-radicalization applications, as an example, lease prolonged counseling, exposure to opportunity viewpoints, and the rebuilding of the man or woman's precise identification. For those people now not at once affected however seeking to defend in opposition to such manipulation, information remains our maximum exceptional weapon. Understanding the mechanics of brainwashing, spotting its signs and symptoms, and having a strong feel of self can offer some degree of safety. In give up, brainwashing is a effective reminder of the human thoughts's fragility. But it additionally underscores our resilience and the first-rate capability to rebuild even after gift way excessive mental trauma. As we navigate our contemporary world, brimming with a deluge of facts and tries at affect, can also we be ever vigilant, significantly analyzing the data we devour, and generally staying real to ourselves.

Case Studies of Mind Control Incidents

Imagine on foot thru the bustling streets of a modern-day metropolitan metropolis. Every face that passes is truely some other stranger, every one preoccupied with their very own lives and issues. But among them, there is probably some who have lived critiques beyond ordinary comprehension, reminiscences that dive into the shadowy realm of mind manipulate. Through those reminiscences, you can come to understand the profound consequences of such practices and learn how to understand the insidious threads of manipulation.

The Tale of Amelia

Amelia, a devoted monetary representative, had generally been seemed for her impartial spirit and steely determination. But over a span of months, her close to pals observed a alternate. She began out attending conferences for a self-assist business enterprise that promised to release her hidden functionality. At first, it appeared innocent. The institution's charismatic chief, Mr. Grey, regarded to provide the keys to enlightenment.

However, as time handed, Amelia have end up more and more isolated from her loved ones, dedicating an increasing number of of her time and sources to Mr. Grey's teachings. Her as soon as-fiery spirit seemed subdued, her movements oddly mechanical. The transition became diffused however unmistakable. The company had employed a mixture of isolation, repetitive teachings,

and an amazing revel in of community to mildew Amelia's wondering.

After almost a three hundred and sixty five days, Amelia's buddies intervened, exposing her to out of doors views and slowly supporting her spoil unfastened. But the scars remained, and the enjoy left her wary, normally on defend closer to any shape of undue affect.

In the Shadows of Power: The Politician's Play

John become a rising celebrity in the political landscape, regarded for his attraction and eloquence. When he became delivered to a manner consultant named Helena, he turn out to be promised modern techniques that might make sure his victory in the upcoming elections.

Helena emerge as adept in intellectual manipulation. She added John to strategies that would sway public opinion with out them know-how they were being caused. Subtle nudges in speeches, use of particular symbols that resonated with deep cultural narratives, or even controlling the tone and tempo of his addresses to elicit precise emotional responses from the audience.

John's advertising campaign soared, however so did his dependence on Helena. She slowly started out to govern no longer certainly his public addresses however additionally his political selections. It modified into high-quality after a whistleblower from his institution determined the depths of Helena's manipulation that John sought assist. The revelations shook his self perception, and he took a step lower once more from politics to heal and mirror.

Chapter 14: The Hidden Aspects Of Nlp And Hypnosis

In the complicated tapestry of human interaction, wherein language paperwork the very threads that weave our social fabric, there lies a realm that sticks out for its profound impact on communication, self-development, and persuasion: Neuro-Linguistic Programming, typically called NLP. For our readers, who're searching for to traverse the labyrinth of dark psychology and emerge with device to navigate private and professional landscapes, information NLP is a key bankruptcy on this odyssey.

The Genesis of NLP

Born in the Nineteen Seventies, NLP modified into the brainchild of Richard Bandler, a pupil of statistics generation, and John Grinder, a linguist. Their blended information introduced about the advent of an area that sought to discover patterns in human behavior and communication. Their proposition changed into radical however intuitive: if one may additionally need to identify patterns in a achievement human beings, they'll be modeled and taught to others, facilitating a switch of these a hit behaviors. This essence of NLP—decoding the form of excellence—

holds big energy, presenting pathways to personal boom and effective communique.

Demystifying the Nomenclature

The very name, Neuro-Linguistic Programming, may additionally seem arcane, however it gives a truthful illustration of its center tenets. 'Neuro' acknowledges our neurological techniques, recognizing the indelible bond amongst our mental and physiological states. 'Linguistic' emphasizes the centrality of language, both verbal and non-verbal, in shaping our mind, behaviors, and interactions. Lastly, 'Programming' is a nod to the idea of behavioral styles and the capability to change or 'reprogram' the ones patterns for added effects.

The Deep Dive into Human Communication

At the coronary coronary heart of NLP lies the exploration of techniques we communicate. Not just with others, however with ourselves. NLP postulates that our internal dialogues shape our perception of truth. For instance, individuals can enjoy the identical occasion but may additionally apprehend, keep in mind, and respond to it in every different way. This variance is attributed to the character 'maps' or 'models' of the place we create primarily based on our reviews, ideals, and values. For our readers, who are positioned on the nexus of private and expert management, information the ones nuances becomes paramount. In a boardroom, for example, while pitching an idea, figuring out that each person operates from their specific map can useful useful resource in tailoring conversation for resonance. Similarly, in non-public spheres, acknowledging those perceptual filters can pave the way for empathetic interactions and battle choice.

NLP's Tools: Anchoring, Reframing, and Rapport

Among the multitude of device NLP gives, three stand out for his or her immediately applicability: anchoring, reframing, and constructing rapport.

Anchoring involves associating an emotional united states of america with a bodily gesture or sign. Think of the elation you may experience paying attention to a selected tune from your kids, transporting you decrease lower back in time. Such establishments, whilst understood, may be purposefully created, presenting a toolkit to rouse favored emotional responses, every in oneself and others.

Reframing, but, is the artwork of changing the that means of an occasion through changing its context. Consider a situation wherein a colleague constantly arrives overdue for conferences. An immediately interpretation might label the colleague as irresponsible. However, reframing would possibly probably present an exchange perspective—likely they're managing a private disaster or coping with a traumatic mission. Such a shift in perception can foster information and collaborative answers.

Lastly, constructing rapport, a cornerstone of NLP, underscores the significance of putting in place connections based totally on mutual understand and records. Mirroring frame language, matching speech styles, and acknowledging shared testimonies can foster a experience of trust, laying the

basis for effective verbal exchange.

The Gray Areas of NLP

While the proponents of NLP champion its transformative potential, it's also important to apprehend its darker factors. In the fingers of a skilled practitioner with manipulative cause, the very gadget of NLP that would empower can also make the most. Anchoring may be misused to trigger horrible feelings; reframing can be wielded to distort truth and validate faux narratives, and rapport-constructing, even as insincere, may be a conduit for deceit.

For our audience, poised on the helm in their personal and professional geographical areas, discernment becomes essential. As one wields the equipment of NLP, ethics need to be the compass. Equally, whilst at the receiving save you, essential wondering and self-cognizance come to be valuable allies, ensuring that one's autonomy stays uncompromised.

In the Landscape of Leadership and Legacy

For our readers, predominantly nestled inside the city heartlands, steerage the deliver in their destinies amidst the dynamic currents of the twenty first century, NLP offers each a beacon and a protect. As leaders, facts the intricacies of NLP can enlarge the impact of verbal exchange, fostering environments of collaboration, innovation, and increase. Yet, with exceptional power comes massive duty. As one harnesses the capacity of NLP, the onus lies in ensuring its

ethical deployment, crafting legacies anchored in authenticity, integrity, and human connection.

In this odyssey thru darkish psychology, wherein shadows often intertwine with light, may also the know-how of Neuro-Linguistic Programming characteristic a guiding superstar, illuminating pathways of actual have an effect on, transformative increase, and enduring management.

Chapter 15: Uncovering The Dark Art Of Persuasion

Dissecting the Mechanism of Persuasion

Persuasion is an ancient art work. From the orators of Athens to the boardrooms of New York, information the ability to sway and impact has usually been a cornerstone of effective conversation. In an age in which mind conflict fiercely for our interest, the mastery of persuasion isn't genuinely an advantage—it is a need. This intrinsic element of human interplay consists of extra than mere terms; it is an complex combination of context, emotion, and cognitive strategies.

In our bustling metropolises, in which each commercial, interplay, and facts article compete for our attention, records the era and art of persuasion becomes paramount. However, in advance than we're capable of absolutely recognize its darker aspects, we want to first dissect the very mechanism of persuasion.

The Dance of Rationality and Emotion

At the coronary heart of persuasion lies the sensitive dance amongst exact judgment and emotion. While we would really like to trust we're rational beings, making picks after careful idea, frequently, our feelings guide our options. Advertisers understand this. The aroma of freshly brewed coffee, a nostalgic song, or a poignant story, are frequently greater compelling than a listing of product talents.

Emotions, which encompass worry, happiness, or maybe anger, may be

effective triggers. For example, a message that inspires fear approximately a capability future event may additionally moreover push us inside the path of a selected selection, even if rationally, the possibilities of that event taking place are minimal. On the turn factor, an enchantment to our happier recollections may also have us associating extraordinary feelings with a selected choice.

However, emotions by myself do no longer seal the deal. Once they have got caught our interest and kindled our feelings, a logical nudge often solidifies our desire. That's wherein rationality comes into play, presenting a comforting explanation to the emotional selections we're leaning in the direction of.

The Role of Social Proof

One of the diffused underpinnings of persuasion is our inherent want to belong, to be part of a collection, and to experience examined. This often manifests in what is termed 'social proof.' When we see others— mainly those we recognize or get hold of as true with—endorsing a notion or motion, we are much more likely to be persuaded via it. In our cities, in which anonymity can every now and then make us sense remoted, this connection, however tenuous, gives a lifeline. Thus, testimonials, endorsements, or maybe the mere perception of popularity can intently tilt our judgment.

Understanding Cognitive Biases

Cognitive biases, those inherent quirks of human psychology, play a high-quality feature in persuasion. For example, the 'affirmation bias' makes us more receptive to facts that aligns with our pre-cutting-edge beliefs. If a piece of facts or an issue fits properly into what we already believe, we're more likely to be persuaded by using the usage of it, regularly overlooking contrary evidence.

Another not unusual bias is the 'availability heuristic.' We have a tendency to be extra stimulated thru the usage of current statistics or sports in our reminiscence, although they are now not the most massive. An event this is sparkling in our minds can unduly have an impact on our choices, making us vulnerable to extremely-modern narratives or dispositions.

The Power of Reciprocity

One of the foundational standards of persuasion is reciprocity. As social creatures, while someone does some thing for us, we obviously need to head again the choice. This precept is clear in our each day lives. A colleague can also propose our idea in a meeting due to the reality we supported theirs closing week. A complimentary dessert at a restaurant can also make us greater inclined to leave a nice compare. Recognizing this inherent tendency can help us differentiate real gestures from the ones aiming to elicit a specific response.

Context and Framing

How a message is framed and the context in which it's provided can dramatically impact its persuasive electricity. In a town putting, the same product might be supplied in a few different way in a immoderate-give up save in preference to a community market. The surroundings, the wording of the monetary, even the lights, can set a context that influences our perception. Moreover, whether or not or no longer a proposition is provided as a loss or a gain, a chance or an opportunity, can trade our response to it.

The Journey Ahead

As we navigate the myriad interactions of our metropolis lives, know-how the mechanism of persuasion turns into an crucial potential. Not virtually to arise to undue have an effect on, but to talk correctly, make informed picks, and be a part of authentically with those spherical us. In a worldwide saturated with messages vying for our attention, being capable of determine the actual from the manipulative, the right from the contrived, isn't always only a skills—it's far a survival tool.

As we keep our adventure, armed with this records, allow us to not view persuasion as a weapon, but as a device. Used ethically, it is able to tell, inspire, or maybe ignite exchange. Used manipulatively, it may mislead, control, and damage. The desire, as continuously, stays inside the fingers of the wielder. But with know-how comes empowerment, and with empowerment comes the capacity to navigate the city jungle with self guarantee, clarity, and right cause.

Unethical Persuasion Tactics

In the bustling city of modern-day society, the paintings of persuasion subtly but constantly permeates the data. Whether we're navigating the agency ladder, deciphering digital media, or maybe really venture each day conversations, persuasive approaches surround us. Yet, like severa art work, persuasion may be wielded with grace and ethics, or it could be misused, essential us into the shadowy realm of unethical persuasion.

To many, persuasion is a tool, a mechanism to collect goals, to persuade mind, or to shift views. But at the identical time as used inappropriately, it transforms from a tool of enlightenment to surely certainly one of entrapment. For our modern-day metropolis audience, inside the age bracket of 35-50, deeply entrenched in each private and professional dynamics, knowledge the nuances of unethical persuasion isn't in reality enlightening—it's miles empowering.

The Illusion of Choice

One of the most not unusual unethical techniques is developing the illusion of choice. Picture this: you are at a store, and a salesclerk offers you two options. Though it seems you have got were given a desire, each options result in the same outcome— shopping a product. This technique subtly corners an person, restricting genuine choice, but leaving them beneath the impact that they made an self sustaining choice.

Exploiting Emotional Vulnerabilities

Another substantially used tactic is playing on emotions. Emotions, being the profound drivers of human conduct they're, can be without difficulty manipulated. A traditional example is the portrayal of best life in advertisements. By projecting a existence of highly-priced, happiness, and achievement, those classified ads play on the innate human preference for betterment, pushing people towards acquisition, often of factors they won't even need.

The Echo Chamber

In ultra-contemporary digital age, specifically in our metropolitan hubs, the echo chamber impact is a powerful unethical persuasion approach. It consists of surrounding an man or woman with best one kind of opinion or mind-set, efficiently drowning out any contrasting voices. Over time, this repeated publicity can mildew a person's perspective, convincing them that this singular view is the precept or even the satisfactory legitimate one.

Anchoring and the Art of the First Impression

Anchoring capitalizes on human psychology. It includes supplying an initial piece of records, which then serves as a benchmark for all subsequent records. For instance, if one is mounted an inflated price first of all and then supplied a slightly decreased one later, they may apprehend it as a good deal, no matter the item's actual simply really worth.

Reciprocity and the Debt of Kindness

Humans are social creatures, and as such, we've got were given an innate choice to repay kindness or favors. Unethical persuaders manage this with the resource of providing some trouble reputedly 'unfastened' or by way of using doing an unasked preference. The seize? It often comes with strings related. The character, feeling indebted, is much more likely to conform with a subsequent request.

Chapter 16: The Role Of Body Language
Decoding the Language of the Body

Amid the labyrinth of conversations, each vocalized and silent, that we've got interplay in each day, lies a powerful undercurrent: the language of the frame. The diffused tilt of a head, the harassed faucet of a foot, or the evasive dart of a watch fixed, all talk volumes. For humans eager on expertise the deeper nuances of human interplay, especially inside the city town of our age, decoding frame language is an artwork, a skills, and every so often, a survival mechanism. As we navigate thru this exploration of body language, envision yourself as a cutting-edge-day Sherlock Holmes, armed with the highbrow prowess to clear up the mysteries encoded in every gesture, posture, and facial functions. Imagine being aware of a talk that, in spite of the fact that silent, reverberates with emotion, reason, and every so often, deceit. The body, much like a ebook, offers a terrific narrative of our inner states. As citizens of bustling metropolitan cities, you've got probably encountered situations in which phrases regarded out of sync with physical cues. A colleague might also additionally moreover assure you of his assist in a challenge, but his folded hands and prevented gaze ought to propose reservations. A friend ought to likely giggle at a shaggy canine tale, however the anxiety in her eyes can also need to betray discomfort. These non-verbal cues are regularly unconscious, making them an actual reflected photo of one's emotions and mind. In the cacophony of metropolis existence, in which each interplay is charged with more than one layers of this means that, knowledge frame language is tantamount to

owning a thriller key. This key unlocks layers of conversation that frequently remain inaccessible to the untrained eye. The electricity dynamics in a boardroom, the unstated tension on a primary date, or the real pleasure of a decide looking their little one—maximum of these scenarios deliver an undercurrent of frame language, revealing more than words must ever deliver.

Why, you can surprise, is frame language so intrinsically tied to our human revel in? The solution lies in our evolutionary data. Long in advance than our ancestors evolved complex languages, they relied on non-verbal cues for communique. Over millennia, as our cognitive abilties improved, so did our repertoire of gestures, facial expressions, and postures. They have turn out to be deeply intertwined with our emotions, reflecting our fears, desires, confidences, and vulnerabilities.

Diving deeper into the matrix of metropolitan interactions, remember the dynamics of a agency negotiation. Two events, seated across a stylish desk, alternate dialogues approximately phrases, conditions, and numbers. But beneath this veneer of formal verbal exchange, a extra profound dance is underway. The organization handshake of one individual exudes self assure, at the same time as the fidgeting of a pen via each different betrays tension. Every pause, lean-in, or look will become a strategic go with the flow, talking reason, gauging reactions, and influencing outcomes.

In private geographical regions too, body language plays a pivotal characteristic. Think approximately romantic pursuits exploring their chemistry on a city midnight. Words may additionally waft in the air, discussing not unusual pursuits, future aspirations, or favored movies. Yet, the actual communique might be taking place inside the interaction of lingering glances, the subconscious mirroring of postures, or the mild contact that lingers a

2d too prolonged. These cues, often disregarded at a conscious level, profoundly have an effect on our feelings, judgments, and choices.

However, as with every powerful tool, body language can be wielded each ethically and manipulatively. A expert manipulator, acquainted with the intricacies of bodily cues, have to feign feelings, assignment fake self warranty, or perhaps prey on someone's vulnerabilities thru studying their non-verbal signs. Such is the double-edged sword of this silent language; it can bridge know-how or be

a device for deceit.

The bustling streets of town landscapes, the immoderate-rises that contact the sky, and the ever-evolving dynamics of present day-day expert and personal relationships are arenas wherein the silent symphony of body language constantly performs. As you traverse your adventure—whether or no longer major a team, forging relationships, or guarding towards manipulations—expertise how to decode the frame's language will now not pleasant provide insights into the human psyche however may also equip you with a profound statistics that transcends words.

For our discerning readers, city dwellers aged 35-50,

popularity at the crossroads of personal aspirations and professional achievements, this exploration is not definitely an academic exercise. It's a compass, guiding you via the labyrinth of human interactions, ensuring you lead, communicate, and live with a intensity of understanding that gadgets you apart.

In last, while phrases live the most apparent shape of conversation, it's far crucial to bear in mind the age-antique adage: Actions communicate louder than terms. In this context, every gesture, posture, and appearance are an motion, revealing layers of reason, emotion, and truth. As you pass beforehand for your metropolitan journey, permit this statistics of frame language be your silent nice buddy, making sure your interactions are as proper as they're insightful.

Chapter 17: Anatomizing Dark Psychological Occurrences

Historical Depictions of Dark Psychology

Dark psychology has not best emerged in our current-day international however has additionally strong its shadow over the annals of records. From the ancient civilizations to the medieval courts, the dance of darkish psychology has left its footprints throughout time, influencing leaders, molding societies, and shaping destinies.

The Ancients and Their Intrigues

To apprehend the intensity of dark psychology's historical roots, we need to tour decrease once more to ancient civilizations, in which political intrigue and courtly drama have been rife. Consider the regal corridors of ancient Egypt. Pharaohs, with their divine proclamations, frequently hired diffused manipulations to solidify their rule. Tales of Cleopatra's beguiling enchantment remind us of the way dark psychological techniques can be hired for every non-public and political earnings. Her alliances, specifically with effective Roman figures like Julius Caesar and Mark Antony, weren't mere whims of passion but calculated actions, pushed through a practical statistics of human psychology.

Journeying to historic Greece, the bedrock of democracy and philosophy, we encounter memories full of darkish intellectual nuances. Greek tragedies, a testomony to their societal dynamics, regularly depicted characters ensnared inside the webs of manipulation, betrayal, and deceit. Oedipus Rex, for

instance, is greater than handiest a sad hero; he is a person subjected to the whims of manipulative forces, each divine and mortal.

Medieval Machinations

As we bypass beforehand in time, the medieval a long time present a tapestry of kingdoms, knights, and narratives in which darkish psychology often played the lead feature. The machinations of courtly politics, with its ever-converting alliances and betrayals, stood as a testomony to the energy of darkish intellectual strategies. Kings and queens, in their quest for power, frequently hired manipulative strategies, exploiting loyalties and emotions.

Shakespeare, together together with his timeless plays, encapsulated the essence of dark psychology in this period. Characters like Lady Macbeth and Iago are not mere fictional entities however emblematic of the depth to which manipulative strategies had been woven into the societal fabric.

Renaissance: A New Dawn, Old Shadows

The renaissance, frequently hailed due to the truth the age of enlightenment and cause, wasn't without dark intellectual undercurrents. The fervor for artwork, era, and literature turned into paralleled through using the extreme political and spiritual dramas unfolding during Europe. The Borgias, an infamous Italian own family, had been emblematic of this age, the use of dark highbrow strategies for electricity and manipulate in the coronary coronary heart of the Holy See.

As artwork flourished, so did depictions of dark psychology.

Artists like Caravaggio didn't shrink back from showcasing the awful realities of human psyche and its susceptibilities.

Colonial Conquests and the Age of Reason

The age of exploration and colonial conquests introduced a new period to dark psychology. Colonial powers, in their quest for contemporary lands, regularly hired manipulative techniques, exploiting neighborhood populations' beliefs and feelings. The promise of alternate, alliances, or maybe faith have been equipment wielded to similarly imperialistic targets.

Concurrently, in the salons of Europe, the Age of Reason become dawning. Philosophers and thinkers dissected human behavior, laying naked the intricacies of the thoughts. Yet, alongside those illuminations, the shadow of dark psychology endured. Works which encompass Machiavelli's "The Prince" supplied insights into the artwork of manipulation, a manual for leaders on wielding electricity through smart mental processes.

Modern Times and The Persistent Shadows

The modern-day era, regardless of its enhancements, hasn't remained untouched by using the use of way of the tendrils of darkish psychology. Industrial magnates, political figures, or maybe celebrities have, over and over, showcased how manipulation can be used to gain goals, have an impact on hundreds, and consolidate power. The

World Wars, at the same time as in large part political and territorial battles, had been moreover theaters of intellectual struggle, wherein international locations sought to demoralize enemies via propaganda and

subversive techniques.

Understanding history isn't quite lots dates and activities; it's far approximately comprehending the undercurrents that inspired those occasions. Dark psychology, with its exciting combination of manipulation, mind manage, and emotional exploitation, has been a normal participant on the ancient degree. Recognizing its function across some time lets in us no longer only apprehend the complexities of past activities however additionally equips us to apprehend its manifestations in our cutting-edge age.

Historical depictions of darkish psychology function a replicate, reflecting humanity's vulnerabilities and the lengths people or entities can go to take advantage of them. They stand as reminders and schooling, urging us to tread with caution, recognition, and the information bestowed with the aid of statistics.

Scrutinizing Manipulation in Media and Governance

In the interconnected age, the have an effect on of media on public sentiment is remarkable, with governance and political systems regularly intertwined on this net. It's important to understand the depth of manipulation that occurs inside the returned of presentations and revealed phrases, to be each knowledgeable and protected.

The Tapestry of Modern Media

Over time, media has advanced from an insignificant tool of records dissemination to an influential entity shaping public perceptions. Radio pronounces once united the loads, tv added visuals into homes, and now, the virtual age immerses us in a in no way-completing motion of facts. But as media's obtain broadened, so did its intricacies.

Imagine a theater. A story plays out on degree, fascinating the target market. Yet, backstage, selections shape the plot, from which person to attention at once to which subplot to bypass over. Similarly, media systems decide which tale to tell, how to inform it, and whose voice narrates it. The functionality for manipulation proper right here is profound. Narratives can be spun to healthy positive agendas, data may be furnished out of context, and emotions may be preyed upon.

The Alchemy of Framing

"Framing" refers to the presentation of an occasion or trouble in a selected mild or context. For instance, a protest might be framed as a "violent uprising" or a "peaceful demonstration for rights." The preference of terms, snap shots, or perhaps the tone of voice can notably modify intention marketplace perception. But it is not quite lots the big recollections. The subtle nudges, the steady biases, and the omnipresent innuendos interwoven into each day statistics have an effect on our perspectives over time.

There's a obligation on media stores to be objective. However, economic pressures, political inclinations, or the race for higher rankings can reason the dilution of this objectivity. It's no longer unusual for facts shops to intensify war or controversy, simply due to the fact "it sells." Thus, information the underlying motivations can offer a clearer view of the landscape.

Governance and the Power Play